Learning Strategies

Routledge Education Books

Advisory editor: John Eggleston
Professor of Education
University of Warwick

Learning Strategies

John Nisbet and Janet Shucksmith

London and New York

First published in 1986 by Routledge & Kegan Paul plc
Reprinted in 1988 and 1991 by
Routledge
11 New Fetter Lane, London EC4P 4EE

Published in the USA by
Routledge
a division of Routledge, Chapman and Hall, Inc.
29 West 35th Street, New York NY 10001

Set in Times, 10 on 11 pt
by Inforum Ltd, Portsmouth
and printed in Great Britain
by St Edmundsbury Press Ltd,
Bury St Edmunds, Suffolk

© *John Nisbet and Janet Shucksmith 1986*

A catalogue record for this book is available from
the British Library
ISBN 0–415–03111–7

Contents

Acknowledgments

The research work which provided the basis for this review and analysis of learning strategies was funded by the Scottish Education Department. The views expressed are those of the authors and do not commit the Department in any respect.

Many teachers and pupils in the Grampian Region generously gave us their cooperation, interest and help. We are especially grateful to Ian Smithers, David Eastwood and Margaret Eletheriou for their support and encouragement throughout. Secondary schools throughout Scotland assisted in the survey of study skills provision. Other researchers, working on related projects, provided stimulating insights; and our Advisory Committee, with J.P. Forsyth as chairman, contributed a helpful critical commentary during the project.
The substantial secretarial work involved in collaborative work with schools and in the preparation of this book was expertly done by Sheila Riach and Margaret Sinclair.

To all of these we wish to express our sincere thanks.

John Nisbet
Janet Shucksmith

Introduction

The most important learning is learning to learn. The most important knowledge is self-knowledge.

Of course, mastering the content of knowledge is important also, for 'learning to learn' and 'self-knowledge' are vacuous phrases if they are not set firmly in a context of experience. The traditional curriculum concentrates on 'useful knowledge' and 'basic skills', on reading, writing, mathematics, practical subjects, science, environmental studies, creative arts and specialist studies. Unfortunately more general strategies of learning such as solving problems, using memory effectively and selecting appropriate methods of working, are often neglected. Study skills courses have been introduced to deal with this aspect in the later years of secondary school or at college or university, or for adults returning to study; but by then it may be too late to change habits which have already become established.

Learning to learn involves learning strategies like planning ahead, monitoring one's performance to identify sources of difficulty, checking, estimating, revision and self-testing. Strategies like these are sometimes taught in school, but children usually do not learn to apply the strategies beyond specific applications in narrowly defined tasks. Effective learning demands more than this: skills and strategies have to be learned in such a way that they can be 'transferred' to fit new problems or situations not previously encountered. Being able to select the appropriate strategy, and to adapt it where necessary, is an important part of this definition of good learning.

Strategies are 'the secret algorithms of learning' (Duffy, 1982). In this book, the term 'strategy' is used to indicate a level above that of skills: strategies are the executive processes which choose, coordinate and apply skills. Strategies are different from skills in that a strategy has a purpose, it is a sequence of activities and it is more readily modified to suit the context, whereas a skill is more specific or 'reflexive'. Understanding the strategies of learning and gaining self-knowledge, in the form of awareness of the processes we use in learning, helps us to control these processes and gives us the opportunity to take responsibility for our own learning.

Thus, learning to learn depends on developing a 'seventh sense', an awareness of one's mental processes. 'Metacognition' is the jargon term which psychologists have recently adopted for this aspect of learning. Cultivating this seventh sense should be one of the prime aims of the curriculum.

This is not a teach-yourself book. It is a book that we hope will be read by teachers and those concerned with the education of primary and secondary school pupils. The aim is to encourage them to start thinking about some different approaches to harnessing the potential of young learners. It is also relevant to adult learners, and to those who teach them. Thus, although it is a book about learning, it is also very much about teaching.

The teaching of study skills, which is reviewed critically in Chapter 2, has developed from the realisation that many students and pupils fall short of their potential because they do not know how to set about the task of study. Some study skills courses are little more than tips for coping with the examination system. Others, however, build on an understanding of the process of learning and aim to encourage self-awareness in the learner.

Chapter 3 examines the broader notion of learning strategies. These provide the means by which we can control and regulate our use of skills in learning. Chapters 4 and 5 discuss this approach in greater detail. How do children develop as learners? Even quite young children show insight into learning strategies, but they lack the ability to use that insight to good purpose: 'Young children can do much more than they will do' (A.L. Brown, 1977).

In Chapters 6, 7 and 8, we bring the strands together to show how these ideas can be translated into classroom practice. Chapter 6 reviews three approaches to improving the capacity to learn: direct training in learning strategies; modelling, where the teacher describes how she works in order to direct attention to the process of learning; and encouraging discussion of metacognitive strategies such as self-monitoring to develop insight into managing one's mental processes. Chapter 7 outlines the practical work which we did over a two-year period with teachers and children, and gives examples of some of the materials which were tried out in schools.

The final chapter reviews the place of learning strategies in the curriculum. Their application is likely to be an evolutionary development, not a revolutionary change. Learning strategies are not a substitute for the traditional approach to the curriculum, or in opposition to it. The two approaches can be combined: indeed, they should not be separated.

1

Learning to Learn

Linda and George are both twenty. They are in the second year of their university studies, and both are doing reasonably well.

Linda is well-organised in her studying. Her friends think she is too preoccupied with her 'system', but being organised comes naturally to her, she says. She acknowledges the influence of her mother, who continued a professional job while raising a family and running a household, and consequently provided Linda with a model of organised efficiency. In fact, Linda was rather the opposite kind of person as a teenager in secondary school, finding difficulty in doing all the things she wanted to squeeze into a busy life. When she realised that she would have to get better results if she wanted to qualify for university entry, she had been impressed by a study methods talk about planning and organising. She started to write out detailed programmes of each day's targets in her diary. That did not last long: it was too inflexible and laborious, besides being disheartening because her targets were too ambitious. But the experience had proved useful, for now she can do this kind of planning in her head, without being too fussy over detail. Give her an assignment – an essay or a piece of reading or a seminar paper to prepare – and she quickly reviews the scale of the task to decide what is required and how much time she should spend on it, and tries to match time and task. She likes to work to a coherent programme, with an awareness of time constraints, for this enables her to phase her work into her other commitments, including her free time. She falls back into a written programme at busy times, before examinations, when pressure mounts.

Watching her at work, you notice that she uses books selectively, glancing through the pages till she finds the passage she wants; she make notes and summarises as she reads; she checks and revises what she has written. Of course, not all her time is as productive as

1

this description suggests. She has a habit of copying out neat versions of drafts, and is aware of this as a time-wasting activity to guard against. But the general impression is that she knows what she is doing and knows how to do it. Reflecting on it, she also realises that her preoccupation with covering the work may sometimes get in the way of a deeper understanding and a more independent, and possibly more interesting, style of study.

Though this systematic approach is now second nature to her, she has in fact learned it, first from her home which provided a model for her, and then from a fortuitous school experience which happened to meet a need which she was only vaguely conscious of. She has learned to monitor her progress, aware of targets and time whether on a long-term task (a project over a whole term or longer) or in an evening's study (with six jobs to be done before an interesting television programme at 10.15). She is still self-consciously practising a routine, but she is not tied to it inflexibly. When she does it intuitively (and afterwards has forgotten that she ever had to learn it), she will have aquired a strategy of working and learning which will be valuable throughout her professional life.

* * * *

George has more natural talent, flair and imagination than Linda, but he is much less a paragon of method. Indeed his style of working is often haphazard, and sometimes chaotic. He prefers to study in spurts, working long hours when he feels in the mood and giving up when he feels he is making no progress. He likes to browse through books, and his reading also is of a casual and unplanned pattern. He does not make notes or summaries from his reading; but he has a powerful memory which provides him with quite an effective retrieval system. (At school, one of his teachers had insisted that he should make notes of his reading, but he had found it an unprofitable practice, merely accumulating scrappy notes which he could never find when he needed them.) In reading books, he is good at getting to the heart of the author's meaning, and consequently he can recall the gist even if he forgets the details.

He disclaims any pattern in his studying. His priorities are decided by what is most urgent, and by what he likes doing best. When the urgency builds up, he can work right through the night; and though he grumbles when he has to do this, there is a certain satisfaction in coping successfully with a crisis.

Most of his friends share the same attitude. He gets on rather better than they do, and his friends attribute this to his intelligence and quick wits. There is more to it than this, however. He has learned to cope with pressure (a useful acquisition), responding to stress by drawing on his reserves of energy. He admits that he lacks the ability to apply himself to his work, explaining this in terms of 'personality'. He uses the word 'personality' as if, at his mature stage of life, it were something to come to terms with, as if he had no choice.

George has in fact acquired a strategy of learning, and it works satisfactorily for him. It is a risk-taking strategy, and he has learned to deal with – and even enjoy – the pressures involved. His use of the strategy is reinforced by the fact that his friends do likewise: unconsciously perhaps, George is influenced by the models of his peers and of older students whose style he admires. But it is not a wholly unreflective strategy. He is sharp enough to recognise that he has to put his ideas together in a framework so that he can readily recall reading and lectures; and he works at this quite seriously, discussing and arguing with his friends until he feels secure in his convictions. This too is a useful strategy which he will continue to develop, building on the strengths of this approach to study. Or perhaps, if he comes to rely too much on scraping through with a last-minute effort, he will slide into sloppy habits of work.

*   *   *   *

Bill and Susan are secondary school pupils. Bill has an essay to write on a contemporary novel. The novel itself was not very interesting, and he skimmed through the later chapters. Fortunately, the teacher had given the class some notes; more important, she had taught them to make rough notes as they read; and as a result he has a usable outline of the plot. Also, in his first year at secondary school, his English teacher had drilled him in a procedure for essay writing: make notes, identify a theme, create a structure (beginning, development, conclusion), use quotations, and so on. He follows this routine for completing his homework essay, and is able to turn in a satisfactory but unimaginative piece of work.

Bill is one of life's plodders, conscientiously looking for and sticking to the one 'right' method of working. It is a strategy which, unfortunately, pays off in many school situations, and he will probably end up with a reasonably good set of grades and a school report which describes him as a 'good student'. His inability to adapt to changing requirements and his lack of self-knowledge may start to be a problem when he is expected to study on his own. But for the present, his teachers do not see him as a problem and are quite glad to have a few like Bill in their classes.

Susan *is* something of a problem to her English teacher, but not in mathematics and science. She is clearly an able girl, imaginative and talented especially in problem-solving exercises which she enjoys doing. She applies herself conscientiously to school work, but her marks in English are poor. Assessment in her English class is based on written work: in class discussion she contributes fluently and intelligently, and this patent evidence of ability adds to her English teacher's feeling of frustration. Susan too has feelings of frustration about her writing and reporting, feelings bordering on alienation. She does not understand why this part of the curriculum is so difficult for her, and she gets no satisfaction from the additional exercises which her teacher sets for her. She is looking forward to the time when she can drop the study of this uncongenial subject and concentrate on those which she is good at.

Can either she or her teachers diagnose the problem? Can they work together to remedy it? Some of the procedures which Bill follows in his unimaginative way provide a starting point: her English teacher has tried this, but there is not the time in a busy school syllabus for following up the exercises with discussion to analyse the difficulties and with encouragement to persevere.

In the meantime Susan is making rapid progress in learning to handle mathematical reasoning. As regards her weakness in writing, she is learning to accept this as a handicap to live with.

*   *   *   *

Tracy, Craig and Karen will soon be leaving primary school. They all are happy at school, but their primary school experience has already established habits and attitudes which will affect their later learning in very different ways.

Tracy is a busy worker, though often she is busy to little purpose. She takes part actively in group work, especially in conversation, but she does not seem to understand what the task demands. Her work is obsessively neat and she takes pains over the appearance of her notebooks (as do her parents). She copies out sections of reference texts tidily for her projects, without being aware whether or not they are relevant. Her writing is fluent and neat, and this tends to obscure its lack of structure and meaning. She tries to guess what the teacher wants: school work is for her, as for many primary school children, a matter of diligent application to meet the requirements imposed by the teacher. Her teacher commends her diligence, but berates her as a chatterbox and silently bemoans the sheep-like way she follows the actions and accepts the ideas of others in her class. Tracy will leave primary school with quite a good report, and she is certainly competent in reading and arithmetic. Probably she will not be 'found out' by the system until she is thirteen or fourteen, when her style of working will begin to prove inadequate.

Craig is fond of reading and has developed a wide range of interests, which he can talk and write about fluently. His parents have encouraged him in this, and in talking with him about his reading they provide him with practical help and a model of their own way of life. They help in a practical way with guidance on how to find interesting books in the local library and encouragement in following up ideas for things to do. The school does this also: school and home together have already given Craig a sound introduction to working with books. However, Craig has trouble with arithmetic. (When he is older, he will have decided that he is no use at maths.) He works too fast and makes many errors. He never checks his work. He frequently uses the wrong method with arithmetic problems, for he has little idea of what the questions require. Thinking about things like that takes time; and when you have twenty sums to do, you attract unwelcome attention if you are the last to finish. So he makes sure that he finishes whatever he is given to do, and this keeps him out of trouble in the arithmetic lessons.

Karen is learning to use a computer. She spends a lot of time sitting at the machine. She reads the instructions for the program and uses trial and error to find her way through the procedure. When she makes a mistake, she repeats the sequence, and then repeats it with different input, testing alternative possibilities. No one has taught her this, but she is intrigued by the machine and is resolved to explore its operation. She is working thoughtfully and systematically according to a mental plan which is at least partially conscious and deliberate. Her teacher is sceptical about computers, for the software seems trivial or irrelevant, and though the children enjoy playing with them – as she describes it – they do not seem to be learning anything. Karen is learning something from the experience, not just how to operate the keyboard but also how to anticipate and check, and her experimenting becomes more efficient and more systematic as the days pass, though she herself is unaware of the change.

*   *   *   *

What are the differences among these learners? And what are the reasons for these differences?

Effective learning is not just a matter of age or years of experience. In the example described in the first part of this chapter, the university students are applying sophisticated strategies in studying, but this is because their work demands this, and Linda and George are examples of the successful survivors in the process of formal education. But many young children set about their learning efficiently – Craig in following his interest in books, Karen working with the computer – and many students labour ineffectively. As adults, most of us avoid the need to learn if we can, by keeping to familiar routines. Faced with an unfamiliar learning task, few of us know how to set about it, like Susan with her writing problems. We tend to fall back on routines which we know, like Bill in his essay writing, even when they are inappropriate. Diligent effort is misplaced if the strategy is wrong, as Tracy and Craig with his sums will soon find out.

Nor is effective learning just a matter of intelligence, unless we define 'intelligence' as the collection of procedures and insights which we have learned. The strategies which George and Linda apply to their university studies have been learned or taught. Even the limited strategies which Bill and Craig use are ones which they have learned to adopt or which are implicit, unintentionally, in the tasks their teachers set. Admittedly, some people are more competent than others in learning appropriate procedures and in applying these appropriately; but some apparently intelligent people can be remarkably unintelligent in their approach to learning – for example, in learning to drive a car or how to diagnose the fault when it won't start, to use a computer, to speak a foreign language, to converse with social skill, to read a map or to remember names or telephone numbers. Each of these competences requires different ways of learning, and 'intelligence' alone will not enable us to master them.

The successful learner is not necessarily the person who has discovered and mastered the 'correct' procedure for each situation. In this book we use the term 'strategies' to refer to integrated sequences of procedures selected with a purpose in view, and successful learners have developed a range of strategies from which they are able to select appropriately and adapt flexibly to meet the needs of a specific situation. To do this, they need to be aware of what they are doing and of their own learning style, and to monitor their learning so as to be able to make appropriate decisions and to switch their choice if it appears to be ineffective. Thus, successful learners are more likely to be those who are fine-tuned to the complexities of their learning style, who are perceptive of the requirements in learning, and who have developed a range of strategies which they can apply according to their own style.

What is it then that distinguishes good learners from poor learners, or even good learning episodes from unsatisfactory learning episodes for each of our characters? It is obviously not merely the possession of a certain intelligence quotient or even a clutch of academic study skills or 'right' methods. What seems to be the pivot of each child's reaction to the learning situation is his or her ability to monitor (consciously or unconsciously) the demands of the task and to respond appropriately – to recognise and manage the learning situation.

This sort of awareness involves a range of what have been termed *metacognitive skills*.

In short, the essential reason for the differences in the examples is that the successful learner is one who has *learned how to learn*. For Linda and George and the others, some of the elements in learning to learn have been taught, and other aspects they have learned for themselves. Whether taught or learned, the elements can be unproductive unless the student or pupil can bring the parts together in a coherent management of the process of learning. Learning to manage the process of learning involves *being aware of what one is doing*, or being able to bring one's mental processes under conscious scrutiny and thus more effectively under control. This awareness of one's mental processes is termed 'metacognition'. Linda in the first example has reached the stage (nearly) of doing it intuitively; Bill writing an essay is quite unable to do it but merely adopts unquestioningly the models he has been given; while Margaret, trying to master the computer's mode of working, is developing a clearer awareness of her own thinking (or at least will do so if she is given prompting and encouragement).

To speak of metacognition in this way, as a sophisticated awareness of one's mental processes, seems to place it far beyond the capacity of primary school children, or indeed of most adults. Of course it can be developed to a highly sophisticated level, but as a form of awareness it accompanies all learning. As Flavell (who invented the term, 'metacognition') pointed out, when I realise that I am having difficulty in learning something, I have entered into metacognition. From there, it is a small step to consider why I am having difficulty, and this sensitivity to method is by no means limited to adults. But this kind of introspection cannot be constantly conscious and deliberate, or we could never learn because of thinking about learning. What is required is an early introduction to the practice of monitoring one's learning, and the capacity to call it into play in deciding how to tackle a task. Though learning is largely intuitive, the learner should be able to move from the intuitive to the deliberate when some difficulty intervenes, stopping to consider the source of the difficulty and to select a strategy to deal with it.

The role of metacognition in learning may be compared to awareness of movement and strategies in sport. The speed, co-ordination and style of top athletes seem to result naturally from their fitness and agility, spontaneously, without a moment's hesitation or thought. But the art of the coach is to make the athletes more aware of their movements and strategies and thus to obtain better control and co-ordination. The newly acquired skill then has to be practised until it becomes intuitive, though it can be retrieved into consciousness when needed.

Following this analogy, we might call metacognition 'the seventh sense'.

7

Traditionally there are five senses. The phrase, 'a sixth sense', is often used to imply some super-sensitivity in a person's awareness. However, the psychologists have appropriated the 'sixth sense' for the more mundane kinaesthetic sense, the awareness of one's bodily movements. My seventh sense is metacognition, the awareness of one's mental processes, the capacity to reflect on how one learns, how to strengthen memory, how to tackle problems systematically – reflection, awareness, understanding, and perhaps ultimately control, the seventh sense is a relatively undeveloped sense among people generally. (Nisbet and Shucksmith, 1984)

How do people acquire this sophistication in learning and in being aware of their mode of thinking? Can one learn how to learn? And can teachers teach how to learn?

The answer is yes, people can learn how to learn. They learn this all the time – more perhaps in childhood because there is so much to learn, but they are always learning whenever something new comes along or old routines prove ineffective: learning to focus attention, to anticipate and hypothesise, to interpret and analyse, to master by repetition and practice, to handle numbers and other abstract symbols, to make notes, to identify key points, and so on. They also learn how to put these skills together, into what we call 'strategies of learning'. Sometimes, the strategies we learn are poor strategies: guessing impulsively in the face of difficulty in the hope that things will become clear later, skipping the difficult parts, memorising details instead of looking for principles. We also learn attitudes, of confidence or anxiety or expecting failure, taking an interest, making persistent effort or risk-taking – the emotional and motivational, affective and conative accompaniments to learning.

How do people acquire this general capacity which we are describing – the capacity to organise their mental processes for learning or problem solving, and the monitoring and control which become possible through awareness of their thinking? They learn it from successful or unsuccessful *experience*, often unconsciously through reinforcement or punishment. They also learn it from *models*, from the examples of other people's ways of learning. The first models are the parents; then teachers and other adults; they also learn from the example of their peers. The capacity can also be developed by *teaching*, as we argue in this book, either by direct instruction or indirectly through metacognition. In fact, learning of this kind is usually haphazard and is left to chance.

At what age does this kind of learning happen? Probably it starts at a very young age. For example, how you set about solving problems, and how you respond to any kind of challenge or difficulty, depend on basic attitudes and responses which begin to be learned in the pre-school years. (This does not mean that you cannot acquire these attitudes or change your mode of response later.) One child may learn to be patient, holding back on impulsiveness; another may acquire the rule that if reasoning does not work try brute force. Or the rule learned may be that if you are not sure, do what others are doing so that you are not conspicuous. Response modes generalise from practical experiences. They may be influenced by physiological factors underlying personality, but in part at least, and probably for the most part, they are a learned response. It is difficult at this age to separate a pattern of response from attitudes and values: for example, risk-taking as a strategy depends on feeling secure and not worrying too much about being wrong.

At a more complex and advanced level, for the learning which underlies adult academic and professional activities, the foundation is probably laid in the early or middle years of adolescence. By this age, children are emerging from the stage of mastering elementary skills, and are now moving into more complex activities. They are more socially responsive, and they encounter a wider range of models for behaviours and values. They are also becoming more sophisticated and thus better able to introspect, to be aware of their own thoughts and to be conscious of their feelings, and thus to be able to plan and control more effectively. But relatively few are able to do these things. Those who do need the help of good models or good training or good luck in their experiences or all of these together.

The 'study skills movement' in secondary schools and colleges is a response to growing recognition of the need to develop the capacity for learning. Initially the teaching of study skills was limited to those going on to higher education, as if it were not necessary for others. It extended to adults returning to study or trying university courses for the first time with the Open University or in continuing education, and those who come from educationally disadvantaged homes. Some study skills courses degenerate into techniques for passing examinations, for coping with the system rather than developing the skills of learning. For many students, the good advice comes too late to be an adequate corrective for wrong habits already well-established by the age of seventeen or older. The task of learning to learn is a continuously developing task, but, in our view, it has a special place in the education of children between ten and fourteen. In these years, for many children, the basis could be laid. By this stage, basic skills have been mastered; these are the early years of adolescence for most young people; there is a marked development in mental functioning, an increased self-awareness

9

and a change from Piaget's concrete operations to formal reasoning. For many, these are the years when an opportunity is missed.

The question is not 'Can teachers teach how to learn?' They do: whether they intend it or not, they are *models* for their pupils in the learning styles and strategies which the teachers use. Secondary school teachers commonly teach skills which are specific to their subjects, and which are implicit in these subjects: science teachers, for example, demonstrate hypothetico-deductive thinking, and English teachers encourage sensitivity to language and clear expression of ideas and feelings. Such task-specific skills seldom generalise to activities beyond the school and subject context. Teachers may teach mnemonics or self-testing as a procedure for memorising, but these tend to remain 'tricks for passing exams'. What is needed is for teachers to build sound learning strategies into their teaching, and to know how to do this in such a way as to encourage transfer to a more general approach to learning.

This has been the subject of our work in recent years, and it is the theme of this book. It is important primarily as a guiding principle in the regular school work of children and young people. It is of relevance for adult learners: with the pace of technological change, the years of compulsory education cannot teach all that will be needed through adult life, and consequently schools must teach for adaptability. If the study skills movement is to make a genuine contribution to people's learning, rather than help to cope with note-taking and examinations, the ideas presented here must be taken into account. Our better understanding of cognitive skills, stimulated by developments in computing and communication, opens up the intriguing possibility of increasing our learning capacity. Perhaps that is too ambitious an aim at this stage: the chapters which follow explore what is involved in learning to learn and aim to translate recent research into a practical curriculum policy for schools. 'Learning Strategies', the title of the book and its central theme, contains a deliberate grammatical ambiguity; but the word 'learning' is first and foremost a verb.

2

Learning to Learn:
The Study Skills Approach

'You teach science; well and good; I am busy fashioning the
tools for its acquisition. . . It is not your business to teach him
the various sciences, but to give him a taste for them and
methods of learning them when this taste is more mature. This
is assuredly a fundamental principle of all good education.'
(Rousseau, *Emile*, 1762, Everyman edition pp. 90 and 134)

Learning to learn is not a new idea. The quotation from Rousseau,
out of context, seems surprisingly modern; but Rousseau aimed to
develop attitudes to and methods of learning separately from
formal teaching, prior to the acquisition of knowledge. Present-day
learning theorists tend to start from the principle that learning to
learn is a capacity to be developed concurrently with the experience
of learning. The teaching of study skills, the topic of this chapter, is
open to criticism for failing to build on this principle. Too often,
study skills are a separate and subsequent 'add-on' element in the
curriculum for older pupils or college students. The students may
learn the rules, but they continue to rely on the habits which they
have already acquired in the course of their previous experience of
learning.

Learning to learn: different approaches

The idea of learning to learn has attracted attention in recent years
from various groups: the advocates of continuing education, curriculum theorists, cognitive psychologists, educational reformers,
and teachers of study skills. Those who campaign for continuing
education argue that 'learning to learn' is a prime aim of the years of
compulsory education: if 'lifelong education' is to be a feature of a
modern technological society, then schools should be concerned

with training young people to be effective learners, with a disposition to carry on learning. Curriculum theorists (such as Hirst, 1965 and Phenix, 1964) suggest that, in a curriculum designed to cover basic forms of knowledge, students or pupils will learn the distinctive modes of thinking.

'Learning to learn' has become a topic of central interest in the area of cognitive psychology, though it is seldom referred to under that title. Information-processing and cybernetics gave a stimulus to this field of research in the 1950s, and significant progress has been made in recent years, especially since 1956, when Bruner, Goodnow and Austin published their seminal text, *A Study of Thinking*. Yet, despite the time and effort expended by psychologists and learning theorists on research into learning, relatively few of the ideas and findings have filtered through into the school curriculum. One reason for this is that much of the research has taken the form of laboratory experiments which lack classroom validity, on limited aspects of psychological theory, often reported in highly technical language.

Various proposals for reform have stressed the idea of 'learning to learn'. The Plowden Report (1967) gave its blessing to the idea in general terms:

> The child is the agent of his own learning. . . We certainly would not wish to undervalue knowledge and facts, but facts are best retained when they are used and understood, when right attitudes to learning are created, when children learn to learn. (Para. 529)

The Welsh version of Plowden, the Gittins Report (1967), was more specific:

> Apart from the essential intellectual and social skills of language and mathematics, it seems to us that the child should 'learn how to learn', be able to seek information when he needs it, and become increasingly independent of his teachers. (Para. 10.3)

Dearden (1976), reviewing the emergence of the idea from 1948 on, defined 'learning to learn' as 'a family of structures of second-order learning, of different kinds of "learning how to learn" related to different general classes of more specific learning'. Five different meanings of this rather unhelpful definition were identified:

1 Learning to learn involves acquiring information-finding skills: learning how to get information on a given topic;
2 Learning to learn means mastering general substantive principles: learning general rules which can be applied to the solution of

a wide range of more particular problems;

3 Learning to learn occurs through understanding the formal principles of inquiry: learning the 'logic' of different forms of inquiry and the methods which have produced findings;

4 Learning to learn refers to developing autonomy in learning: the self-management of one's learning activities;

5 Learning to learn is essentially a matter of attitude or approach: it involves cultivating a 'habitual disposition which is intrinsically rewarding'.

Even this further analysis leaves teachers uncertain as to how to promote the 'learning to learn' which they are urged to develop.

Learning to learn: study skills

The solution which schools have tended to adopt is the provision of courses on study skills, and this is the approach with which the present chapter is concerned. The study skills movement has grown apace in recent years, at first in the universities in the 1950s from concern over student failure and subsequently in the senior classes of secondary education as schools recognised the difficulties faced by 'first generation students' who were now staying on beyond age sixteen in increasing numbers. The foundation of the Open University in 1969 provided a further stimulus as a new type of adult student was recruited to higher education, and there is now a flood of manuals on 'how to study'.

In Britain, one of the most influential books was a best-seller in the immediate post-war years, Bruce Truscot's *First Year at the University* (1946). This was a 'user-friendly' text, explaining to a new generation of students what university education was all about. After an introductory chapter, 'What is a university?', the book offers advice on a range of topics: organisation (Chapter 4), concentration and memory (Chapter 5), examinations (Chapter 6), reading (Chapter 7) and even friendships and courtships (Chapter 9). This set a pattern of coverage which many of the subsequent manuals followed.

But in education each generation rediscovers the wheel; the idea of advice on study methods goes back much further in history. In 1741, Isaac Watts (composer of hymns such as 'O God, our help in ages past') published *The Improvement of the Mind*, a collection of advice based on his own experience as a scholar (see Entwistle, 1981, pp. 32–37, for extracts). Between 1900 and 1924 at least fifteen manuals on study were published: Hinsdale's *The Art of Study*, 1900, is one of the earliest, and others include Earhart's

Teaching Children to Study, 1909; Dearborn's *How to Learn Easily*, 1918; and Thomas's *Training for Effective Study*, 1922. Reading through these old texts is an illuminating experience. Comparing them with present-day manuals, the reader is impressed, first, by the superior presentation and lay-out of modern texts, and second, by the astonishing similarity in content and actual advice. The style changes but the advice remains the same. The pattern seems to have been established by about 1924, when the Bureau of Educational Research at the University of Illinois published a sixty-six-page bulletin, *Training in the Technique of Study* (Monroe, 1924). There, the advice begins:

> Successful study is difficult in a room which is not warm, well-lighted, well-ventilated and otherwise comfortable. . . The first step is to provide a physical environment which will not interfere with effective study.

Sixty years later, writers of some manuals are still preoccupied with the physical environment as 'the first step'. In the 1924 bulletin, subsequent rules follow a familiar pattern: 'Make out a daily schedule. . . Before you start studying, collect all the texts you will need. . . Begin working as soon as you sit down. . .' The common 'deficiencies in study procedure' are:

1 Inability to read textbook material . . .
2 Study conceived as a process of memorizing . . .
3 Failure to organize and summarize . . .
4 Failure to review . . .
5 Lack of a regular time and place for study
and so on.

In 1949 Laycock and Russell published a summary of thirty-eight such manuals. Today there are over a hundred in print, and many of these repeat the advice unchanged. This would not matter if we could be sure that the advice was sound. But much of it seems to lack an empirical base, and it has very little connection with recent work in cognitive psychology. To quote Maddox (1962), it is largely 'self-perpetuating material based on general consensus'.

> Most of the advice on learning and remembering is more applicable to rote-learning than to meaningful learning: in particular the usual advice on recitation, interference, over-learning and the distribution of practice. Advice on acquiring motives and developing concentration tends to be merely hortatory and ineffective because it lacks detail and specificity.

(Maddox was himself the author of a most successful manual on study in 1963: the paper from which the above quotation is taken was never published in full.) The most telling criticism of this conventional advice is that many of the most successful students do not adopt the recommended procedures.

A further criticism of the way in which study skills are taught is that they are too often presented in isolation, separately from the actual studying and learning with which the students are faced. In this respect, Monroe's 1924 publication is more modern than many of the manuals which followed in the fashion. It urges that

> training in study procedure should be based upon an understanding of the individual needs of the pupils concerned, should be designed for specific purposes, and should be planned with care . . . never treated as incidental.

It also recommends that training in study methods should be done by the classroom teacher: 'It is necessary that the training be such as may be given in connection with the classroom instruction.' The point (though awkwardly expressed) is the same as the conclusion from the recent NFER survey by Tabberer and Allman (1983) – a principle not observed in most of the study skills provision:

> At its least satisfactory, it (teaching study skills) may become merely an additional subject within the curriculum, quite isolated from other subjects to be learned. . . It may be better conceived as the provision of support for the study problems that students already encounter in their subject classes. To achieve this, its content and approach must be closely linked to the actual problems that students have, and its organisation must be carefully planned to augment the teaching and learning which students already regard as important.

A survey of study skills provision

To establish the range and variety of provision of advice to school pupils on methods of study, a brief questionnaire was sent to all the 431 secondary schools in Scotland. The headteachers were asked to let us know whether the schools provided such advice, and if so, which years were given it (S1/S2, the first two years; S3/S4, the middle years up to O-grade examinations; S5/S6, the years beyond the minimum leaving age). They were asked two questions only: 'Does your school arrange short courses on methods of study? Or are there discussion classes where study methods are a specific topic of discussion?' The response slip was simple, with spaces for replies separately for S1/S2, S3/S4 and S5/S6 and a space for comment. An accompanying note invited the teachers to send more detailed information if they wished, and promised to report back to them the results of the survey.

150 schools responded, and many added helpful notes about their provision. (Some of those from schools in our local area, the Grampian Region, were followed up by visits and interviews.) 23 schools replied that they made no provision; and if we can assume that the non-responders also did not make any formal provision, the remaining 127 (nearly 30 per cent) provide an outline of current practice.

The different forms of advice on study methods were classified in four categories:

A short courses;
B discussion groups;
C class work with the guidance teacher, or as part of a social education course;
D incidentally in class work with subject teachers.

As many schools used more than one of these methods, the analysis of replies became complex. A simple count of numbers is clearly an inadequate method of reporting but is a convenient starting point (see Figure 1).

100 schools made formal provision for advice on study methods:

(i)   50 provided short courses: 25 courses only (A)
                                   10 courses and discussion
                                      (A+B)
                                    7 courses and guidance/social
                                      education (A+C)
                                    8 all three approaches
                                      (A+B+C)
(ii)   59 used discussion groups 21 discussion only (B)
        (18 of which are included 20 discussion and guidance/
        in (i) above):   social education (B+C)
(iii)   44 provided advice through 9 as part of guidance/social
        the guidance teacher or as   education only (C)
        part of social education
        (35 of which are included
        in (i) and (ii) above):
(iv)   27 replied that study skills were covered incidentally in class
        by subject teachers.

The older pupils were the main target for this advice, but 17 of the 100 schools arranged some kind of course for the pupils in the first two years of secondary school, and 24 (including 4 of the 17) arranged discussion of study methods for these pupils. For the third and fourth year pupils, 11 schools arranged courses, and 44 (including 8 of the 11) arranged discussion groups. For the fifth and sixth year pupils, 28 schools arranged discussion groups. These figures

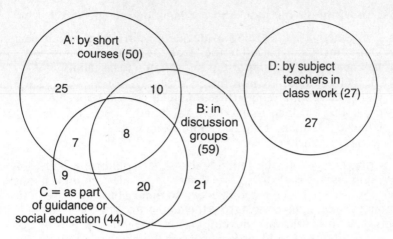

Figure 1   *How study skills were taught in 127 secondary schools*

probably give an over-estimate of provision, in spite of the number of non-responders, because several of the 'courses' amounted only to a single talk by the head teacher or an outside speaker or a video film, and the discussion likewise was limited in some cases, as was clear from our follow-up inquiries.

In summary, about one in five of the secondary schools in Scotland made some provision for advice on study skills, mainly for older pupils (though one in ten made some provision for the youngest pupils). Not surprisingly, the topic was generally seen as most appropriate to those years when public examinations tend to dominate the curriculum. A few schools stated that tuition in study skills was reserved for those who expressed a firm intention to continue into tertiary education. Since a number of schools furnished information about their courses, it was possible to identify common themes. These could perhaps be characterised as representing ways of coping with the school system rather than techniques for learning:

1 Responsible use of study time, the right environment, pacing study and revision;
2 Homework discipline, encouraged by regular use of homework diaries;
3 Note-taking from lessons or lectures and from reading;
4 Presentation of material in course work;
5 Revision methods for examinations.

However, there were 27 schools which responded that the topic was dealt with only within the context of regular class work, even though the format of the questions did not mention this specifically.

> Study methods or learning strategies are carried out within each
> Department and it is left to the Head of Department as to how
> he imparts this very important information to his pupils.
> Methods of Study are introduced at all stages of our work. They
> will be dealt with frequently and fully, but *not* as a specific
> topic. I feel strongly that to have a slot in the academic year
> labelled 'Methods of Study' is both sterile and
> counterproductive.

Leaving the task to the individual teacher could be a 'fall-back
position': it is possible to assume that one is inculcating study habits
or learning strategies without ever examining the validity of this
assumption. It is impossible from the replies to distinguish precisely
between those who are developing an integrated provision for
teaching study skills and those who are making no specific provision
at all. Difficulties may arise from a policy in which 'it is left to the
Head of Department. . .'. Advice from one department may sometimes contradict another where there is no overall agreement on
what constitutes 'good study patterns', or where some teachers
interpret study skills as little more than academic housekeeping.
Marland (1981) complains:

> Learning to learn is rarely specified as a curriculum aim. . . It
> seems to be presumed by those planning school syllabuses that
> the processes will be assimilated while subjects are being
> studied.

Nevertheless there are some schools where there is a coherent
policy to develop a general competence in learning in the context of
the work which the pupils are doing in their regular classes.

Building on study skills

Teaching study skills is not the same as 'learning to learn', even
when they are embedded in regular learning tasks in classroom
work. The difficulty is that study skills taught within a subject context may be too specifically tied to the subject, and consequently are
not readily transferred to related situations in other subjects. General
advice, on the other hand, may be too vague to be applied in any
specific context. There is a solution between these two extremes,
which is developed in the chapters which follow. A clearer understanding of what is involved in study skills could enable teachers to
apply techniques more explicitly in classroom situations, and to
demonstrate their transferability to other new situations. From the

learners' viewpoint, this is a switch of emphasis from specific skills connected with school subjects towards an approach which aims to teach the learners to understand themselves. Thus, for students or pupils, the essential value of discussion about study is to raise their awareness of methods of learning and eventually to lead them to a conscious development of their own learning strategies.

This approach is built into some of the more recent study manuals and some school practices, for example, the book by Hamblin (1981) on *Teaching Study Skills* and the 'Lifeskills' project (Hopson and Scally, 1980) which aim to teach study skills within the context of guidance and counselling. The risk in this approach is that the whole topic may be tipped into the bin-end of social education classes which have still to establish their legitimacy and relevance – at least, in some schools – in the view of both teachers and pupils. If this happens, the result is that the topic remains as peripheral to the curriculum as any of the old study skills programmes.

Marland's Schools Council project on *Information Skills in the Secondary Curriculum* placed its guidance on gathering and handling information in a much wider context:

> The emphasis is on information and study skills within the secondary curriculum, but the general principles certainly apply to learning tasks given to pupils and students of all ages. . . (p.7). Learning to learn is not only part of the curriculum in its own right: given a whole-school approach it is also a powerful aid to improving the effectiveness of the rest of the curriculum. (p.43)

The report of the project (Marland, 1981) identifies nine steps which pupils should follow in completing an assignment. What do I need to do? Where could I go? How do I get the information? Which resources shall I use? How shall I use the resources? What should I make a record of? Have I got the information I need? How should I present it? What have I achieved? Each of these steps is elaborated by further questions and suggestions, detailing choices, procedures and criteria for decision. Teachers are urged to use the nine questions as 'a framework for discussing the steps to be followed':

> While younger pupils can be offered specific techniques, older and more experienced pupils . . . can be encouraged to try out a range of techniques, to assess the purposes to which a technique might usefully be put, and to discuss their study approaches with one another. (p.48)
> If there is a single element underlying this discussion, it is that *how* pupils learn is just as important as *what* they learn. (p.42)

The Open University text by Smith (1983), *Learning How to Learn*, is another example of advice on study skills set in the context of 'direct links to application': the subtitle of the book is 'Applied Theory for Adults'. In fact, much of the text is general advice of the kind found in other conventional study manuals. It specifies rules for different kinds of learning: self-directed learning, learning collaboratively, learning from teachers and 'alternative ways of learning' (from radio, television and 'every day experience'). It differs from other manuals, however, in stressing that students should aim at 'self-understanding' and at becoming more aware of the processes and procedures in learning. This awareness is cultivated through 'constructive self-examination':

> A central task of learning how to learn is developing awareness of oneself as learner. . . Self-understanding links directly to learning how to learn when learners become sensitive to, and in control of, the learning processes. . . It may be done unconsciously when one reflects on an experience (processes it) or consciously when, for example, instructors provide feedback concerning the how of learning as well as the what. (p.57)

This is a different style of approach from the usual rule-book style of books on 'How to study', and it is much closer to the approach which we intend to analyse in later chapters. But the process itself, of self-understanding or awareness or whatever one calls it, needs to be spelt out more fully, and this is difficult because the ideas are amorphous unless they are expressed in the technical jargon of cognitive psychology. Moreover, the link between such awareness and learning how to learn is not as simple as may be assumed, but requires appropriate practice and possibly models to copy if students or pupils are to learn to put the ideas into practice. Otherwise learners tend to see the generalisations as merely peripheral to their 'real' work, and the impact is lost. Embedding the generalisations in specific subject tasks is not a solution in itself, for students also have to develop the capacity for 'transfer', so that they can apply what has been learned in one context to another different but analogous situation.

The problem of transfer

'These study skills courses are pointless,' argues the teacher, 'if the pupils can't remember to use the good habits or techniques when I give them a real problem to solve in my own lesson.'

'What's the use of learning skills like appreciation of audience or register,' queries the parent, 'when he can't work out how to open his mouth at an interview.'

'Skills training is ineffectual,' says the psychologist, 'if the skill is retained only for use in the context in which it was learned but cannot be generalised or transferred to new problems or novel situations.'

The concept of 'transfer' or generalisability introduces a complication into the business of learning to apply the skills which one has learned. Tabberer and Allman (1983) reviewed many study skills programmes in secondary schools and concluded that a major deficiency in most of them was that skills were taught out of context, in courses which ran parallel to the everyday school curriculum but meshed with it only rarely. If study skills are taught out of context, they are unlikely to be applied in practice. Teaching the skills within the context of regular subject teaching, on the other hand, limits the capacity for transfer. Checking, for example, may be learned and applied in computation, but a pupil may find the principle less easy to apply to essay writing or French translation. This is 'the skills dilemma'. The problem in both of these contrasting approaches is not so much a lack of knowledge of skills, but an inability to apply them. It is a 'production deficiency', in that learners cannot produce the appropriate skill when faced by a novel problem or unfamiliar situation. The instruction may improve pupils' knowledge about study methods without improving their general efficiency in studying, because pupils do not or cannot apply the skills. They are unable to select an appropriate procedure, even though they may 'know' a range of methods to choose from.

If transfer is to be the criterion for establishing the success of skills training, then it is obvious not only that skills must be taught in a meaningful context, but also that they must be taught with transfer in mind. This is how 'the skills dilemma' is to be resolved. Teaching for transfer implies bringing the transferable elements – concepts and principles – into consciousness, and pointing to their more general applicability.

Learning to learn in primary education

At what stage of education can this be introduced? The wording of the last sentence in the previous paragraph suggests that the kind of teaching and learning involved in study skills is appropriate only to a sophisticated college-level student, or to the selected classes at the upper end of the secondary school. These are in fact the age groups towards whom most instruction in study methods is directed. But earlier in this chapter it was suggested that the reason for this is that

21

this is the age when students find they have to be more autonomous in their learning and when examinations loom large, and many study skills courses are little more than advice in how to pass examinations and satisfy the requirements of an academic school system. If study skills are not introduced into the curriculum until after age sixteen, this may prove too late to be effective. By that age, learners have already worked out for themselves the habits which they prefer – and the survivors in college and sixth form are those who have done this successfully. Not all of their established practices will necessarily be the most appropriate, but it is too late to change when the pressures of study are already weighing heavily on them. They may listen to the advice on study, but they continue to use the practices which they have used so far.

Advice on study methods was first given to university students, and then to the senior years of secondary school. The survey reported above showed that advice of this kind is now seen (by some schools) as necessary for first-year pupils entering secondary school, obviously in a different style from what is given to college students. Perhaps the starting point is in the primary school? (Some might argue that the foundation is laid in the pre-school years, where children use parents as models to learn from intuitively.) Within primary education there is a trend to teach skills within 'learning modes' such as speaking, listening and reading, and in environmental studies and primary school science. These skills, however, are restricted to specific areas of the curriculum, and have to struggle to survive against the dominance of the traditional 'basic skills' of primary education. They are also linked in a simplistic fashion to the concept of children's developmental stages, in that it is the children's intellectual development which leads to the mastery of skills rather than vice versa.

On the analogy of Bruner's (1965) hypothesis 'that any subject can be taught effectively in some intellectually honest form to any child at any stage of development', it seems that there is a place for making a start with learning to learn in the primary school. But how is this to be done? What is the 'intellectually honest form' appropriate to this age? This is a question to which we return in later chapters. Our own hypothesis is that the learning strategies approach is one which is especially applicable at the later stages of primary school when children are beginning to develop greater self-awareness. 'Learning strategies' is a mid-way concept between the abstract generalisations of study skills courses and the specific subject-linked techniques of learning currently taught, and may thus provide a way to resolve the 'skills dilemma'.

Summary

The study skills movement has gained momentum in recent years, but can be criticised on six counts.

1 It lacks a theoretical basis, having no link with developments in cognitive psychology.
2 It lacks an empirical basis, being based on a self-perpetuating consensus.
3 It is often too general and out of context, so that it is not seen by learners as relevant to their needs and so is not applied.
4 It is not transferable, being often a collection of tips for coping with specific subject-based procedures.
5 It can too readily become merely a way of coping with the formal requirements of the school system, particularly with passing examinations.
6 It is too late, in that habits are already formed by age sixteen or eighteen.

However, there is a widely perceived need for something of this kind, and some recently published texts point the way to a more effective way of developing study skills. This approach builds on an understanding of the process of learning and encourages greater self-awareness in the learner. It also requires teaching for transfer. In this way, a beginning can be found for learning to learn.

3

What are Learning Strategies?

A definition and an analogy

It is something of a cliché now to quote the passage from Alice in Wonderland where Humpty Dumpty maintains that words can mean whatever he chooses them to mean, but it is a principle that seems to have guided many of those engaged in educational research. Perhaps it is inevitable that concepts which are new and which are still being explored should be continually redefined by each user, but it can be confusing for the reader. Two of the terms used in this chapter – 'learning strategies' and 'metacognition' – have been used variably and ambiguously; so it will be worth our while to spend a little time at this stage defining fairly clearly what we understand a learning strategy to be. We hope that the definition of 'metacognition' will grow out of the explanation as the chapter progresses.

What are learning strategies? A simple answer is that strategies are the processes that underlie performance on thinking tasks – but this explanation does not take us very far. A simple analogy with a football team and its trainer might take us further towards an explanation. Much of the team's time in their practice sessions will be taken up with exercises to improve the players' skills at dribbling, tackling, ball control and so on. These separate skills might be discussed back in the dressing room in front of a blackboard, planning moves that the team could build up against their next opponents. One plan is for the ball to be passed to the left wing, where the player who receives it will make a twenty-yard sprint up the wing before passing it back into the centre. Our first player will have made enough ground to pick up the ball and will lob it high for a third man to head into goal. This string of skills built together might be labelled a tactic or strategy: it is a series of skills used with a particular purpose in mind. But let us extend the definition by carrying the analogy a little further.

The tactic outlined relies on the trainer's knowledge that his player on the wing is particularly fast and that he has an attacking player in mid-field who always uses his head well. In their next match our team has the misfortune to meet opponents who mark particularly closely on the left wing and whose defenders are so tall that they win every ball that goes into the air. A poor team might persist in their original tactic regardless, with ever-diminishing success. A good team should be able to monitor the new situation, revise its tactics and redeploy its skills. The decision to do so might come from the players themselves or from the trainer at half-time.

How does the trainer encourage this quality in his team? Not by constantly exercising their skills so that they sprint faster, pass more accurately or tackle with more flair. Not even by piecing these skills together in even more sophisticated blackboard moves. Each of these may play a part in a training programme, but there is a quality of flexibility, awareness and imagination which the team will need in order to put these skills and tactics together in response to a problem on the field. This is what we mean by talking about strategic thinking.

Analogies can be misleading, but this one says something about why many of the school programmes which teach more and more specifically differentiated skills and sub-skills are only ever likely to be partially successful. The acquisition and improvement of those skills may be an essential part of the school experience, but the factor which differentiates good from bad or inadequate learning is the ability to monitor situations, tasks and problems and respond accordingly, and this is an ability too rarely taught or encouraged in school.

An example from the classroom

What can we distil from our illustration of 'strategy': what lessons might we want to draw from it about school learning? Strategies are more than simple sequences or agglomerations of skills; they go beyond the 'strings' or routines advocated in some study manuals. They are almost always purposeful and goal-orientated, but perhaps not always carried out at a conscious or deliberate level. They can be lengthy or so rapid in execution that it is impossible to recapture, recall or even be aware that one has used a strategy.

Consider a typical school situation where the class teacher decides that one of the topics on the syllabus should be carried out in the form of project work. She wants the finished projects to represent more than just a 'cut-and-paste' exercise, so she spends some time preparing her class by talking about the various skills they will need. In particular she reminds them how to locate books in the school library, emphasises the use of the index in reference books and lays down clear guidelines about presentation. She even pins to the wall a poster she has made stating the eight steps she wants the class to follow in their search for and presentation of information. She is a good teacher and, with a few exceptions, the class exercise the skills she has encouraged. Yet not all the finished projects will be of equal merit. The members of the class will not all have learned the same things from the experience. What criteria for the exercise will our teacher have set in deciding whether individuals have performed satisfactorily? One of them may well be that the material collected should be relevant to the topic or question. She has provided them with certain skills for finding relevant information (knowledge of library layout and catalogue, use of book index), but the difference between the good and poorer projects will lie in each child's ability to assess and monitor the relevance of each piece of information found to the demands of the task. In presenting their work the good learners will bear in mind more than just the physical constraints of layout and length that the teacher has set. They will (probably unconsciously) monitor their work, plan their collection of information in line with the aim of the task, check their progress, revise their estimate of what they are going to be able to achieve and examine and test their final product before handing it in for formal assessment by the teacher. Probably none of these super-ordinate skills or strategies will have been taught or even mentioned by the teacher. The better pupils may do some of them instinctively and probably unconsciously if the teacher has made her aims clear enough. It may never cross the minds of the poorer pupils that those 'super-skills' are necessary.

With this classroom example we are perhaps coming closer to a definition of 'strategy' which is useful to the teacher. Strategies seem to represent higher-order skills which control and regulate the more task-specific or more practical skills. They seem to be more general in nature, the sorts of activities (like planning and checking) that are going to be needed time and time again in all sorts of different situations and problems.

Naming strategies

We can attempt to make this difference between skills and strategies a little clearer perhaps by looking at the way different authors have visualised the learning process. In particular it is interesting to see the different names or labels that they attach to the superordinate skills or strategies. Which of them will have the best application to our classroom situations?

Resnick and Beck (1976) tried to emphasise the difference by talking about *general strategies* when they meant broad activities connected with reasoning and thinking and *mediational strategies* when they were referring to the specific skills or 'tricks' that we use when completing a task.

Sternberg (1983) is more specific. He distinguishes between *executive* skills – 'the kinds of skills used in planning, monitoring and revising strategies for task performance' – and *non-executive skills* – 'the skills used in actually carrying out task performance'. Thus examples of executive skills would include problem identification, monitoring problem solutions, being sensitive to feedback and so on; Sternberg suggests a list of nine in all. The lower-order non-executive skills are represented by activities like 'mapping' and 'comparison'. Sternberg makes the point that 'both kinds of skills are necessary for high-quality task performance'.

Butterfield and Belmont have used a similar distinction in setting up major training programmes and research projects in America. They plumped for training *executive functions* instead of particular skills, or *control processes* (1977):

> . . .The control processes are seen to be the operations by which we work upon the information available, or retrieve it from memory in order to perform a cognitive task. By contrast, the executive function is the means by which we select, sequence, evaluate, revise or abandon these operations. Thus control processes (or sequences of them) are the goal-directed tactics of cognition; their deployment is the objective outcome of executive planning and revision.

Feuerstein (1979) has also had considerable publicity for his Instrumental Enrichment (IE) program, which makes a similar distinction between skill and strategy levels. He does not exclude the role of non-executive processing, but the main emphasis is on remediating learning deficiencies by a training in broader strategies. The sorts of problems noted in the poor learners whom the programme attempted to help are an inability to select relevant versus irrelevant cues in defining a problem and a lack of spontaneous comparative behaviour.

Using these sources we can draw together a list of the most commonly mentioned strategies. Table 1 gives six of the strategies most frequently mentioned, though they are often found under different names. The list is far from exhaustive, but represents a

typical spread of the super-skills or strategies which might commonly be needed to carry out a school task well.

Table 1   *A list of commonly mentioned strategies*

a	Asking questions:	defining hypotheses, establishing aims and parameters of a task, discovering audience, relating task to previous work, etc.
b	Planning:	deciding on tactics and timetables, reduction of task or problem into components: what physical or mental skills are necessary?
c	Monitoring:	continuous attempt to match efforts, answers and discoveries to initial questions or purposes
d	Checking:	preliminary assessment of performance and results
e	Revising:	may be simple re-drafting or re-calculation or may involve setting of revised goals
f	Self-testing:	final self-assessment both of results and performance on task

A hierarchy of strategies

This dichotomy between strategies and skills remarked upon by so
many authors is easier to maintain in theory than in practice, as
Kirby notes (1984). He makes the same distinction:

> A strategy is essentially a method for approaching a task, or
> more generally attaining a goal. Each strategy would call upon a
> variety of processes in the course of its operation.

However, he finds it useful to postulate a division into *micro-
strategies*, which are more task specific, more related to particular
knowledge and abilities, which are closer to performance and more
responsive to instruction, and *macro-strategies* – a more pervasive
group, often entwined with emotional and motivational factors,
more related to cultural and stylistic differences and consequently
more difficult to change by instruction. It is not necessary to see this
as a dichotomy. One can imagine a continuum instead, reaching
from the most task-specific skills through to the most generalised of
strategies.

A similar notion has often been expressed by authors, implicitly if
not explicitly, in the form of a hierarchy of strategies. Brown (1974),
for example, sees the whole concept of strategies revolving around
the idea of *planfulness* as a central strategy. From her work with

mental retardates and young children she concluded that the chief problem which characterised their poor or immature learning habits was an absence of any intention to make a plan; such children could sometimes perform adequately when carefully instructed but they rarely set out to use a strategy spontaneously.

Baron (1978) uses this central notion to derive a hierarchy based on the ability of the strategies to be generalised. He feels that three principal groups of strategies stem from or hang on this central notion. The first – *relatedness search* – consists of the strategy for searching one's memory for items related to the new problem. This might involve deciding what type of problem it was, what other information or data it was related to and so on. We might see this as similar to our category of strategies labelled 'asking questions'. His second group is called '*stimulus analysis*'. By this Baron means the sorts of strategies by which a problem or task is analysed into its constituent parts. We can see this as similar to our 'planning' strategy in Table 1. Baron's third category of strategy is labelled '*checking*'. He described it as the 'strategy of withholding the first response that comes to mind and continuing to use whatever knowledge one has to try to decide on a correct response'. We could see all of the final four entries in Table 1 subsumed under this heading.

This notion of a structure or hierarchy of strategies is important only in so far as it might indicate the limits (temporary or permanent) to the types of strategies that can be trained. This is a notion discussed further in the next chapter when children's age is considered in relation to ability and strategy use, but for now we might want to alter our original table in line with the notion that not all strategies are equal in either their generalisability or their instructability.

If we accept 'planfulness' as a central strategy, we might also have to accept that while probably not immutable, it may be a characteristic closely related to style or approach to learning and thus extremely difficult to influence. Attitudinal and motivational factors may play an important role at this level. Perhaps the only direct way of influencing this central strategy (at least in an institutional context) is via counselling. At the other end of our hierarchy are the microstrategies. Less generalisable and more task-specific, they are at least easier to instruct. Enlightened teaching methods can make considerable headway in training these strategies as procedures which learners can adopt to encourage a more efficient approach to problems and tasks.

In the middle of our hierarchy, however, come the macrostrategies. These are highly generalisable, seem to improve with age (or at least with experience) and are all characterised by the demands they make upon the learner's knowledge of himself and his own thinking and learning aptitudes and problems. For this latter reason they are often linked with ideas on metacognition. Strategies at this level may be instructable, but are likely to demand something other than traditional methods of training to encourage their development. For this reason they have hitherto been ignored by most bodies concerned with training and learning despite the fact that they may be the pivot or key to the learning process. These 'mind-management' strategies will probably determine the success with which micro-strategies and skills are acquired and used, and may hold a clue to altering the central affective and motivational characteristics of the learner. The next section looks at the place and importance of these strategies which are controlled by our metacognitive knowledge.

Table 2   *A hierarchy of strategies*

	Characteristics	Examples
Central strategy (style, approach to learning)	Related to attitude and motivational factors	'Planfulness'
Macro-strategies (executive processes closely linked to cognitive knowledge)	Highly generalisable Improve with age Improve with experience Can be improved by training, but difficult?	Monitoring Checking Revising Self-testing
Micro-strategies (executive processes)	Less generalisable Easier to instruct Form continuum with higher-order skills More task-specific	Asking questions Planning

Strategies and metacognition

The word given in the literature to the capacity 'to know about one's own knowing', to think and reflect on how one will react or has reacted to a problem or task is *metacognition*. John Flavell is credited with the introduction of the term 'metacognition' in 1970, and he remains the most prolific and respected author on the subject. In 1976, he described metacognition thus:

'Metacognition' refers to one's knowledge concerning one's own cognitive processes and products or anything related to them e.g. the learning-relevant properties of information or data. For example, I am engaging in metacognition (metamemory, metalearning, meta-attention, metalanguage, or whatever) if I notice that I am having more trouble learning A than B; if it strikes me that I should double-check C before accepting it as a fact; if it occurs to me that I had better scrutinise each and every alternative in any multiple-choice type task situation before deciding which is the best one; if I sense that I had better make a note of D because I may forget it . . . Metacognition refers, among other things, to the active monitoring and consequent regulation and orchestration of these processes in relation to the cognitive objects on which they bear, usually in the service of some concrete goal or objective.

The idea of metacognition attracted a great deal of attention from learning theorists in the 1970s. Some disliked the profusion of 'metas' and the introduction of even more jargon, but many welcomed the focus of attention that this re-naming brought about. A great deal of new research was spawned, not all of it clearly thought out. Criticism grew of the sloppy thinking and careless methods that were used to investigate metacognition. Even adherents of the idea began to grow disenchanted at the lack of demonstrable progress made in research studies. Metacognition was in great danger of being 'hoist by its own petard'.

Over the last four years, however, a series of thoughtfully argued theoretical documents have salvaged the hulk of the metacognitive idea, have stripped it down, re-defined it and rebuilt it in a way which makes sense of past discoveries, which links metacognition with other mainstream ideas on intellectual growth and development and which sets it on course for further exploration.

Chief amongst the early critics of metacognitive work were Cavanaugh and Borkowski (1980). They challenged the assumption that cognition and metacognition were linked. They pointed out that children who knew about and could talk about their ways of thinking and learning often performed quite badly on actual thinking tasks. Conversely children who betrayed little or no sophisticated metacognitive knowledge were sometimes found to perform perfectly adequately when given a problem. What was the reason for this lack of congruence? Several possibilities suggested themselves. Either there was no direct link between cognition and knowledge about cognition (metacognition), or alternatively, perhaps research methods were badly flawed and the subtle links between the two were somehow being missed.

Wellman's (1981) answer to this puzzle was that the initial

concept of metacognition was too 'fuzzy' and ill-defined. It was a term that contained within it so many different meanings that it was little wonder that people were having difficulty discerning simple relationships between metacognition and cognition. He pointed out that to some people metacognition referred to *factual knowledge about cognition* (knowing that recall is harder than recognition or that organised lists are easier to remember than unorganised ones). Others used the terms to describe *cognitive feelings or affective* assessments and reactions, such as puzzlement about the outcome of a problem or elation at a successful cognitive endeavour. To many, metacognition implied the *intelligent employment of cognition* in the sense of deliberately using a cognitive skill or strategy towards a particular end, like remembering a complicated list. You will see that all of these definitions are contained in the original passage quoted from Flavell.

Wellman thought no worse of metacognition for it being a 'fuzzy' concept. He pointed out that terms like 'memory' have long been used in precisely the same ill-defined way without hindering understanding or hampering research. His conclusion, however, was that metacognition was essentially a form of knowledge, and as such was no different from any other knowledge one possesses. Its distinguishing feature was its referent – the human information processing system.

Cavanaugh repeated his doubts about metacognition in a paper with Perlmutter in 1982. They reiterated Wellman's point about the 'fuzziness' of the concept, criticising researchers for their failure to distinguish between knowledge about cognition and the processes orchestrating this knowledge. Their suggestion was that the inclusion of executive processes or strategies in the definition was counterproductive. The two ideas needed separating out if either was to have any clarity.

Flavell and Wellman (1977) set out a model of cognition which, though expressed in terms of memory, may serve to clarify the explanation of what metacognition entails. They distinguished four broad but partially overlapping categories of cognitive phenomena:

1 The most basic operations and processes of cognition e.g. the processes by which an object is recognised, the process of cueing or association by which one thing calls to mind a related thing. We may not be conscious of the working of those processes; they probably develop very little with age. Flavell and Wellman have nicknamed this primary or primitive facility of the memory *hardware*.

2 The second category deals with the relatively direct, involuntary, and usually unconscious effects of one's attained level of general

cognitive development on one's memory behaviour. This is termed the *knowledge* component. Obviously it does improve with age as advances in the content and structure of semantic or conceptual systems render inputs more familiar, meaningful and inter-related. This knowledge component of memory is probably as unconscious and automatic as operations in the first category.

3 The third category in this taxonomy introduces the concept of potentially conscious behaviours. Flavell and Wellman labelled these *strategies*. Brown (1978) distinguished between these second and third categories by labelling them respectively 'know-ing' and 'knowing how to know'. Flavell and Wellman illustrated the difference by referring to an adult dog, which may possess both *hardware* and *knowledge*, but which is unlikely to manifest the strategic behaviour illustrated by everyday examples from the human world, e.g. mentally rehearsing someone's number during the brief journey from telephone book to telephone, attempting to reconstruct the day's events in order to remember when and where you might have mislaid your pen.

4 The fourth category would be called, in Brown's terms 'knowing about knowing'. Flavell and Wellman called it *metacognition*. In the context of memory this refers to the individual's knowledge of and awareness of memory, or of anything pertinent to storage and retrieval.

This fourfold scheme serves an important purpose in addition to defining metacognition more clearly, for it sets up interesting questions. Is development of strategy contingent upon the presence of a certain level of knowledge? Can metacognition be used as a tool to foster superior strategies? This last question, of course, is the one that concerns us here, re-emphasising as it does the often observed weakness of the connection between cognition and metacognition.

Why would an individual who knows about a particular strategy not use that knowledge? That is the same question put simply by Cavanaugh and Perlmutter (1982). Their own tentative answer was that too much research had concentrated on assessing the extent of children's knowledge about their cognitions without assessing the effect of other stimuli, instructions and contexts on that knowledge. Wellman (1981) illustrates the problem in relation to a memory task:

> For example, the person could know that organisation is an effective tactic but think that this list is so easy that it only requires quick inspection; the person may recognise that organisation is useful if asked about it but be unable to think of it on his/her own; he/she may use organisation when being strategic but the tasks fail to evoke strategic activity at all; and so on.

What are learning strategies?

This question of the effect of context and stimuli in invoking metacognition and hence strategic activity is crucial to us as we consider the usefulness of these ideas in the classroom. The following chapter tackles the question of how much metacognitive knowledge is linked to age and development, but it is worth remembering that possession of the knowledge is no guarantee that it will be used. Too often classroom contexts and school activities stifle or squash metacognitive and strategic activity rather than encourage it.

Summary

In this chapter we have tried to look beyond traditional notions of study skills to the broader notion of learning strategies. Task-specific skills are an essential part of learning and doing, but too often formal education neglects the executive processes which control and regulate the use of skills in learning tasks or problems. We have called these executive processes learning strategies and have attempted to establish a preliminary list of the sorts of processes which might be involved in school learning tasks.

We have discussed the idea that not all of the processes termed strategies are equal in terms of their generalisability or the ease with which they can be acquired. If we think in terms of some sort of hierarchy, then the sorts of strategies in which we are particularly interested are the 'macrostrategies', related to the use of metacognition. These seem to be the pivot of the learning process, controlling the use of the microstrategies and skills and influencing the character of the learner's overall style or approach.

Metacognition concerns knowledge of one's own mental processes. This awareness is an essential ingredient of many of the strategic activities in which we are interested. We do not know clearly how thought and action are linked in this context. There seem to be well-attested links between cognition and knowledge about cognition, but it would be foolish to expect there always to be a simple and direct relationship between the two, when so many features of the context in which problems or activities are set can distort that relationship.

4
Young Learners: Knowledge and Strategies

So far we have really only speculated about the existence of learning strategies in theoretical terms. The sort of model we have produced linking skills, strategies and metacognition has a value as a way of reducing the complexity of the learning experience and offering us a different perspective. The question remains as to whether it also has any utility in the real world. Can the concepts of learning strategies and metacognition tell us any more about the real learner and his problems?

John Holt has never used the words 'metacognition' and 'strategies', yet he illustrates very well how useful the concepts might be in improving classroom learning. In his book *How Children Fail* (1964) he states:

> Part of being a good student is learning to be aware of one's own mind and the degree of one's own understanding. The good student may be one who often says that he does not understand, simply because he keeps a constant check on his understanding. The poor student who does not, so to speak, watch himself trying to understand, does not know most of the time whether he understands or not. Thus the problem is not to get students to ask us what they don't know; the problem is to make them aware of the difference between what they know and what they don't.

Holt goes on to illustrate this point with an anecdote concerning a child faced with the task of listing verbs that ended with a 'p'. While her classmates got on with the task she became more and more distressed, repeating simply 'I don't get it,' when she was asked if she had a problem. She was quite unable to say what she didn't understand until Holt intervened and asked her if she knew what a verb was. Once the problem had been analysed, the solution was easy to find and the child got on with her work. Holt's comment was:

> She did not know herself that she did not know. All she knew was that she had been told to start doing something and she didn't know what to do. She was wholly incapable of analysing the instructions, finding out what part of them made sense and what did not, where her knowledge ended and her ignorance began.

How can we fit together these ideas about learning strategies and metacognition in a way that makes sense in the classroom? Can we use the idea of learning strategies to bring about more effective learning? Learning is essentially an interactive process. In the classroom the actions and characteristics of both teacher and taught will determine the quality of the learning that takes place. In this chapter we start by looking at the characteristics of children learning. We leave to the following chapter the question of how we can help children to develop more effective learning strategies. Then we look at the teacher's role in setting up appropriate learning situations.

Finding out what the learner knows

Do children act strategically at a young age, or is this something that only develops as they reach their teens? The hypothesis advanced in this chapter is that children already begin to develop metacognitive knowledge or awareness which could control their strategic activities while they are still in the primary school. If, for example, we find such awareness in *some* young children and not in others, this may imply that more effective learning strategies could be grafted on to the usual learning behaviours of *all* children. Perhaps the primary years are too good an opportunity to be missed in terms of changing learning habits; or are we foolish to attempt to influence children when they are too young developmentally to appreciate our efforts? A great deal of metacognitive research has centred on discussion about the changes in the pattern and capacity of children's thinking as they grow older. This is partly because the earlier research interest of Flavell (the 'author' of metacognition) were in replicating and exploring the Piagetian and neo-Piagetian notions of 'stages' in children's development.

A major problem encountered in this research concerns the methods used to discover metacognitive knowledge or to discern the strategies used for thinking tasks. The most frequently used method is that of self-report based on introspection. In other words the child is usually given a task to do or a problem to solve; the child is then encouraged to tell the experimenter either during or at the end of the exercise what methods he or she used. The extent of his metacognitive knowledge about the demands of the task, his own capacities and his performance are elicited by a series of probing oral questions requiring the child to introspect. The drawbacks of using this as the main research method are obvious and legion. We might, for instance, merely be tapping the child's linguistic competencies rather than his metacognitive abilities. John might know more than he can say, his vocabulary being inadequate for expressing abstract thoughts.

One answer to this problem has been to try to back up this simple method by more complex tests in which actions are designed to reveal strategies. For instance, Wellman (1977, 1981) and Yussen and Bird (1979) developed a nonverbal technique for assessing children's knowledge about using their memories. Instead of presenting memory problems verbally, they were presented as a series of pictures. In the first picture, for example, a girl can be seen trying to learn the names of five people; in the next a girl is trying to learn the names of fifteen people, and so on. The child subject of the experiment would be asked to demonstrate comparative judgments about the easiness or difficulty of the tasks by rank-ordering the pictures.

An indirect approach to identifying children's modes of thinking is the analysis of the *errors* which they make in reasoning. For this purpose researchers have tried to devise critical tests or exercises which will reveal children's strategies, especially through errors made.

Another technique sometimes used to back up introspection when working amongst children is that of peer tutoring. Cavanaugh and Perlmutter (1982) report the work of Best and Ornster, who taught a new memory strategy to a group of children who then taught it to a second group of children. 'The measure of metamemory (their awareness of the processes involved) was the amount and type of information taught'. This technique has the advantage that most children are highly motivated by the task of teaching others and there is very little need for the experimenter to intervene or probe, but of course we have no way of knowing whether children are expressing all they know about strategies and thinking in this situation.

The answer suggested by Cavanaugh and Perlmutter is that no single technique can provide a means of entry to the child's mind. In their analysis they discuss a range of techniques that can be and have been used to elicit the degrees of children's metacognitive knowledge and actions. To improve the reliability of data about metacognition these authors suggest that a number of techniques be used together to provide 'converging measures of the variable of interest'.

The development of metacognitive knowledge

Allowing for the inadequacies of research method, what do we think we have discovered about the ability of children at different ages to behave strategically? What do we know about the extent of their metacognitive knowlege? A version of a model first developed by Flavell (1981) may help to answer these questions (see Figure 2).

The arrows between the categories in Figure 2, indicate the interaction between different aspects of cognition and metacognition. For instance, the arrow from cognitive goals to metacognitive knowledge is meant to indicate that the actual selection and formulation of a particular goal can have the effect of retrieving (or activating) parts of one's stored metacognitive knowledge which are considered relevant to that goal. Flavell gives the example of a man trying to understand how to get to a friend's house by listening to her directions.

> Past experience with such problems may have built up a fund of metacognitive knowledge that . . . this goal evokes. Examples might include the knowledge that you are particularly inept at generating spatial representations from verbal directions (person variables), that the number and nature of the steps in her directions will affect the difficulty of your comprehension and memory task (task variables) and that verifying your grasp of the instructions by repeating them back to her before driving off into the night might be a useful thing to do (strategy variables).

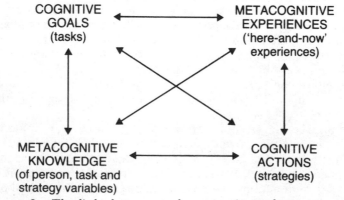

Figure 2   *The links between tasks, strategies and metacognition*

There is much to learn about the factors that make some cognitive tasks harder than others. For example, in a memory task some bodies of information are harder to store and retrieve than others. Units of information that are easily encoded (or labelled or imaged) or which are meaningful and familiar will normally be easier to remember than units which are not. Information which can be related in some way to previously known information is more likely to be successfully stored and more easily retrieved. Children seem to develop quite early an understanding of the effects such task variables will have on their cognitive performance, though their knowledge may be patchy. Tenney (1975), for example, was interested in knowing whether children were capable of estimating the difficulty of lists of items to be learned by rote. He asked kindergarten children, eight-year olds and eleven-years olds to compose lists of words that would be easy for them to recall. The younger children's lists were often random and showed no organisation, whereas the older children tended to organise their words into categories. Most studies show an obvious developmental trend in children's ability to perceive the complexity of a task under different conditions, though their knowledge is far from infallible. Children will often maintain, for example, that a string of objects shown to them in a set of coloured pictures would be easier to remember than the same objects shown in black and white.

Knowledge of the 'person variables' (or personal attributes) has two facets, namely, knowledge of one's own enduring abilities and traits, (knowing, for example, that you are good at handling numbers or bad at remembering names), and knowledge of transient processes and states (becoming aware of a difficulty or a success in learning) – the 'here and now' of cognitive processing shown in the top right-hand corner of Figure 2. Studies have shown that older children have a clearer and more accurate conception of their own cognitive abilities and limitations than do younger children.

The third element in Figure 2, metacognitive knowledge, is a knowledge about strategies. Most studies indicate that as children grow older, there is an improvement in both the range and sophistication of strategies which they can describe. Michael Lawson (1980) comments:

> For normal children increasing age is accompanied by greater awareness of strategies and their likely outcomes, improved accuracy of prediction about performance and better estimates of individual memory capabilities.

Lawson attempted to assess this knowledge even with very young children by simple questioning, asking kindergarten children and young primary pupils how they would remember to bring their skates to school.

In any given task or learning situation it is unlikely that an individual would regard these variables separately. The essence of sophisticated metacognitive activity is the ability to juggle and balance these aspects interactively. Flavell (1981) points out that an individual would know that the ease with which a quantity of information was remembered would depend on the person doing the remembering (person × task). He would know the importance of tailoring his strategies in line with the demands of the task (strategy × task), and, being aware of his own strengths and weaknesses, would choose a strategy that suited his own learning style (person × strategy).

Knowledge into actions: using strategies

So much for metacognitive knowledge: children seem to possess it in large degree. But does this mean that they are able to use it? We have already noted in the previous chapter that there is often a gross mismatch between cognition and metacognition – that is, between the amount people know about their own cognition and their demonstrated use of that knowledge. Nowhere is this more true than amongst children. Ann Brown (1977) has observed that all the evidence points to the fact that children have what she terms 'production deficiencies'. In other words, children's metacognitive knowledge develops before or faster than their ability to utilise that knowledge spontaneously. Most children can perform a strategy when asked or directed, but will act as if they do not possess this knowledge when given an appropriate task or problem. She comments:

> Quite simply, young children can do much more than they will do; it is as if they assign some function of their executive to external agents. Thus many of the familiar mnemonic techniques, rehearsal, organisation, elaboration, etc., are within the child's problem-solving capacity long before he uses them spontaneously.

Children might be able to select categorisation and rehearsal as effective tactics for remembering a stack of pictures, but given the same stack of pictures they might be happy just to look through them.

Flavell (1981) thought that the secret of this production deficiency rested in a change with age in the ability to respond to cognitive goals. The sophisticated learner changes his cognitive actions according to his understanding of cognitive goals: the growing child learns this flexibility only slowly. Flavell offers three possibilities why this may be so:

1 An increase with age in the sheer amount of knowledge acquired and stored;
2 An improvement with age in the organisation and generalisation of knowledge;
3 An improvement with age in the retrieval routes between cognitive goals and metacognitive knowledge.

Thus, in Flavell's view the older child has a greater quantity of metacognitive information to work on, a better library catalogue for quick and efficient access to that information and a developing ability to use that information strategically in the pursuit of cognitive goals.

An example of the 'deficits' that occur is given by Ann Brown (1980) in discussing the strategies used during a reading exercise. A sample of the metacognitive strategies which you, as an adult reader, for instance, are currently employing while reading this chapter includes:

1 Clarifying the purposes of reading – understanding implicit and explicit task demands;
2 Identifying the aspects of a message that are important;
3 Allocating attention so that concentration can be focussed on the major content area rather than trivia;
4 Monitoring ongoing activities to determine whether comprehension is occurring;
5 Engaging in review and self-interrogation to determine which goals are being achieved;
6 Taking corrective action when failures in comprehension are detected.
7 Recovering from disruptions and distractions.

That these processes are automatic for the competent reader is a measure of the years of practice you have had, though the more difficult the text, the less likely it would be that these checking and monitoring strategies would operate automatically or efficiently. Children are inevitably less practised as readers, and it is not unusual for them to be faced with text containing vocabulary or structures of which they have little or no experience.

'Metacognitive deficiencies are the problem of the novice', in Brown's words (1980), and thus we find that 'in general, children fail to consider their behaviour against sensible criteria, they follow instructions blindly, and they are deficient in self-questioning skills that would enable them to determine these inadequacies.'

Elsewhere, Brown (1978) has commented that children not only know less than adults and have less organised and structured knowledge, but that 'they also lack the complex systems of inferential reasoning used by adults to infer information from incomplete and contradictory knowledge bases'. Thus most adults realise immediately that they cannot know Charles Dickens's phone number (Norman, 1973): children have more difficulty working out which bits of this problem they either have information on or could get information about. They have a problem of *metacomprehension* similar to the girl described in John Holt's anecdote at the start of this chapter – they do not know when they know or what they know in the face of a task.

Thus though children may possess a certain amount of metacognitive 'knowledge' at one level, their lack of metacomprehension (not knowing when or what they know) often causes them to fail. The 'triggers' that would bring knowledge and strategies into play fail to operate.

In sum we are fairly sure that children's knowledge about the different facets of cognition and their knowledge of strategies develops at an early age and continues to grow as they approach adolescence. What seems to be absent in young children, however, is the ability to utilise that knowledge and produce those strategies spontaneously when faced with a cognitive goal.

The reasons for this 'production deficiency', it is suggested, lie mainly in the 'novice' status of most children approaching a task or problem. They have encountered the problem-type less frequently than most adults, and therefore have fewer triggers that send them searching their stores of knowledge about cognition and strategies.

Summary

In this chapter we have attempted to see whether work on metacognition and learning strategies tells us anything about the way in which children develop as learners. A great deal of research still needs to be done to find out the rate at which the learner gains more self-awareness of his own learning process. Results so far indicate that even quite young children possess a considerable degree of metacognitive knowledge and that this develops gradually with age. This knowledge consists of information and ideas about the comparative difficulty of different types of tasks, of knowledge about themselves as learners and of the ways in which learners generally operate strategically.

What does not develop either as fast or as inevitably is the ability to use that knowledge strategically themselves in pursuance of a cognitive goal. In Brown's words (1977), 'young children *can* do much more than they *will* do.' This gap between knowing and doing has been labelled as *'production deficiency'*.

The reasons for this production deficiency remain hypothetical. Flavell (1981) characterises the problem as one of inability to respond to cognitive goals. In other words, children have problems diagnosing task-types, and problems matching the assigned task with any of their library of strategies or techniques.

Are we to infer that it is sheer experience – simply the accumulated weight and detail of knowledge, the number of similar problems encountered in the past – that gives the older learner the advantage? On this view, the accumulated experience of situations and problems enables multiple encoding and storage of information so that older learners can more rapidly retrieve and utilise their knowledge.

An alternative interpretation of the improvement in children's mental capacities as they grow older attributes the change to physical and physiological development. It seems likely that the process of physical growth imposes limits on the way in which children can respond to the demands made on their cognition. But experience is also an important factor. This raises the question whether there are ways of sidestepping the seeming inevitability of these developmental trends and intervening to train children in the use of strategies which enable learners to match knowledge with goals.

5

Improving Understanding

The last chapter looked at the way in which metacognitive knowledge develops in young learners and at the way in which that knowledge starts to be used to orchestrate learning strategies. In this chapter we attempt to look beyond these simple generalisations about age and development and to take into account other factors of the learning context.

G. Brown (1984) has made the point that it would be wasteful if the metacognitive debate were to become bogged down in the same arguments about age and performance as have bedevilled discussion of Piagetian 'stage' theory. The need, he claims, is to look at the *dynamics* of that development in children. The learning context is the source of their dynamics.

Setting the learning in context and showing how learning takes place is the sort of argument that must have particular appeal for the teacher. It would be encouraging to think that children's development and achievement were not wholly pre-determined according to their age (mental or chronological) but that development and achievement could be influenced by what teachers and parents can do; but relatively little research has been done in this area. This is illustrated by Brown's comment, reviewing a text on metacognition edited by Siegler (1978):

> Siegler's authors . . . answered the question 'Children's
> Thinking – What Develops?' with the response 'Metacognition
> Develops'. Had the question continued 'And how?' the book
> would probably not have been much longer.

One popular notion put forward is that the first step in a new learning experience is the discovery that there is a problem to be solved and that you do not have the correct solution nor do you know how to solve it. In other words, awareness of your ignorance is the first step towards true learning. In the terminology of cognitive psychology, we could say that metacomprehension is the key which enables us to gain new knowledge and strategies.

This chapter looks at whether it is sufficient simply to induce this 'sense of not knowing' in children, and argues that it is wrong to assume that new learning necessarily emerges from the experience. Instead it is probably necessary to couple this strategy with one in which guidance is offered in some form. Several models are suggested that might offer some insights as to how this could be done.

Knowing that you don't know

In the absence of firm evidence it has often been postulated, not least by Jean Piaget in his early works (1928, 1932), that cognitive advance would be most likely to take place in a situation of conflict where a child's notions, patterns of working, or problem solutions were challenged. This awareness of conflict or difficulty – realising that one's existing knowing or mode of working is inadequate – is an example of what the psychologists call *metacomprehension*: the child is 'ready' for learning when he is made to know that he does not know. French studies as recently as 1981 claim to have tested and endorsed Piaget's conflict hypothesis. Mugny, Perret-Clermont and Doise (1981), for example, concluded, in technical language:

> The subject is emotionally activated when he is involved in interpersonal conflict. He becomes aware of the existence of different centrations, and must come to view his own centration individually.

This theory or hypothesis about learning lies implicit or hidden in some of the teaching procedures that one finds in schools today, although teachers may not recognise it as their aim in setting up learning situations and exercises. Group work in the primary schools, especially in problem-solving situations, based on mathematics and science, leans heavily on the assumptions that peer interaction will produce conflicts of opinion, that the 'right' answer will emerge naturally as the best solution among those offered from the group because it works most often or best, and, of course, that all members of the group will come to accept the right solution and will thus have made an advance.

A less obvious but more common way in which the notion of conflict or challenge forms part of the everyday teaching menu in schools surely lies in the teachers' habit of setting exercises to practise and test knowledge or skills and then marking the answers correct or incorrect with little attempt to diagnose the type of errors made, or to comment on the ease or difficulty of the challenge that the pupil has faced. However, challenge or conflict in this simplistic form – simply being told that you're wrong – does not always create conditions for learning, in the sense of knowing that you don't know, and does not necessarily result in a desire to learn.

Consider the example quoted by Russell (1981, 1982a,b) of a Piagetian problem-solving task: here two boys are arguing about the amount of water in a jar, and one boy is a 'conserver' and the other is not. The conflict theory proves invalid, because when this situation is observed in the classroom it is clear that the less sophisticated non-conserver may see nothing contradictory in his partner's point of view. Russell's point is that many non-conservers do not appreciate that judgments can be objectively true or false. They feel that it is quite possible to have personal preferences for a solution and that both can be right at the same time: ' "You think it's more, I think it's less" is treated in a similar way to "You like that one, I like this one".' (Robinson, 1983). In other words, conflict between peers alone may not be sufficient in itself to engender any awareness that there is a problem. The non-conserver still does not know that he does not know.

Nor do we have any evidence that if our non-conserver could be brought to a state of metacomprehension – that is, if he could be convinced that his thinking was inadequate and that a problem did exist – he would then be able to make the cognitive advance necessary to resolve the conflict. The idea however is an old one in teaching, as Margaret Donaldson (1978) proves by describing the practice of one of the most famous of teachers, Socrates. Plato in the *Meno* describes how Socrates gave a slave boy a lesson in geometry:

> The slave boy came to the lesson with the false belief that if you doubled the area of a square you thereby doubled the length of its sides. Thus if a square, 2 feet by 2 feet has an area of 4 square feet, then another square of twice the area, namely 8 square feet, will have sides of twice the length, namely 4 feet.

Socrates proceeds, by a succession of questions, to lead the slave boy into self-contradiction. The boy then acknowledges that his original belief was wrong and that he does not know how long the sides of the new square will have to be if the area is to be double. When this point in the lesson is reached, Socrates makes the following comment:

> At the beginning he did not know the side of the square of 8 (square) feet. Nor indeed does he know it now, but then he thought he knew it and answered boldly as was appropriate – he

felt no perplexity. Now however he does feel perplexed. Not only does he not know the answer – he doesn't even think he knows.

In other words the slave boy is now *aware* of his error. Socrates goes on to argue that, by perplexing the boy, he has put him in a stronger position for now the boy will want to know. So long as he thought he knew, there was clearly no hope of change, for he was satisfied with his state.

Elizabeth Robinson (1983), however, re-states the dilemma:

> The important point here is that exposing children to what from the adult point of view would be an inadequacy in their way of thinking, may not be sufficient for children to become aware of that inadequacy. Even if children do become aware, that awareness may or may not have developmental significance. And even if it is of developmental significance, it remains to explain why children come to think in a more advanced way rather than just remaining puzzled.

From other work on children's communication skills it seems clear that if conflict operates at all as a mechanism for change, it operates first to induce a metacognitive *experience* (the here-and-now experience in the top right hand corner of Figure 2) – a sense of bewilderment, anxiety or frustration in a child faced with a problem. However, that experience may not be transformed into *knowledge*: the child may still not know that he or she is thinking wrongly until told explicitly. Even then, he or she is a long way from using that knowledge to develop a strategy to resolve the problem.

More seriously, this conflict or challenge model which operates to induce the sense of knowing that you don't know does not form the first step in a new learning experience for some children. For many, especially those who have had the most frequent experience of difficulties in learning, the sense of bewilderment is never resolved. These children do not learn how to use errors and false moves to diagnose and resolve problems. For them errors are destructive rather than constructive. Often the pattern of right and wrong answers seems so arbitrary that they begin to accept that learning is as difficult to control as the weather, and that its regulation lies outside their competence. It is a small step from this point to the one where the only strategies which the child is keen on developing are those which allow him or her to keep out of the teacher's eye.

Showing how to learn

Simply generating an awareness of not knowing does not

47

automatically lead on to learning. The 'metacognitive experience' (see Figure 2) needs to be transformed into knowledge and usable strategies by the actions of the teacher. One way in which this can be done is by the teacher 'modelling' learning in front of the pupils.

An example of modelling in an informal situation is the preschool child learning from his or her parents. Most of the learning that goes on in this situation is unstructured, informal and based on the child using the parent as a model. There is some evidence to suggest that the way in which parents interact with their children at home has a significant influence on children's ability to be reflective about their state of knowledge. Beveridge and Dunn (1980), for example, suggested that there is a 'package' of behaviours which some mothers adopt which has a high correlation with this sort of reflective behaviour in their children. In effect these mothers have a high priority on conversations with their children about motives, feelings and intentions. A similar naturalistic study by Light (1979) offered much the same conclusions and encouraged Robinson and Robinson (1982) to attempt a more controlled study.

Young children commonly do not understand that messages can be ambiguous. The belief on which the experiment was based was that mothers who bother to tell their children they do not understand (when the child has delivered an ambiguous message) are more likely to find that their children develop a keener awareness of meaning. In practice most adults interacting with young children at home, in playgrounds and in the early years of school often fail to pick up and correct the ambiguity. Robinson and Robinson's controlled way of testing this theory was to take 36 four-to five-years olds and give them 6 half-hour 'training' sessions. All of the children practiced listening and speaking in small groups with the experimenter modelling appropriate behaviour. In addition half of the children were also given information about when and why listeners understood or failed to understand them (metacognitive guidance) during the course of the sessions. All of the children in this little test showed improvements in how they performed and understood, but the guidance group improved much more than those who had only had practice.

However, although this 'metacognitive guidance' may be a powerful way of influencing the pattern of young children's behaviour subsequently, it probably occurs quite rarely in real life. Robinson and Robinson's (1982) data showed how rarely such explicit information passes between parents and children. A study by Silbereisen and Claar (1982) makes a similar point in an experiment in which two groups of children were all given a little game or problem to do. One group was left to sort things out on its own. In the other group parents were present and were allowed to interfere and speak with their children to guide them to a correct solution or way of doing the game. Silbereisen and Claar found that many parents were quite unable to offer explicit metacognitive guidance – they couldn't explain to their children where their thinking was wrong, nor could they explain clearly how they should be acting or thinking. Most of the help they offered was in the form of vague statements, such as 'You have to tell it the right way'.

Robinson makes the point in a later article (1983) that it is not clear whether it is the information itself that is important or the behaviour – the interaction – that goes on between the speaker and the listener. In a sense the listener throws the responsibility on the young speaker to make himself understood. Is this more important than anything that is actually said between them? The underlying mechanism in modelling involve more than mere copying.

Brown and Campione (1979) in their studies of mothers and children also note that modelling can provide metacognitive guidance, beyond the explicit content of verbal prompts. Their studies of mother-child pairs working on problem-solving show a gradual weaning of the child from regulation by others to regulation by self. At first the mother controls the child's executive processes and models strategies, but gradually she steps back and allows the child to assume this function for himself. In school situations, as was noted in Chapter 4, young children, though having the knowledge and capacity to execute strategies, often abandon the control and regulation of those strategies to someone else: they wait for instruction and prompts rather than acting on their own initiative.

A tradition of Russian psychology makes very similar claims. Vygotsky (1962), for instance, suggested that internalisation of verbal commands was a critical step in the child's development of the voluntary control of his behaviour. Supporting studies provide evidence for this view, observing a pattern of development like the following:

Early development:	speech of adult controls and directs child's behaviour
Later development:	child's own *overt* speech becomes an effective regulator of child's behaviour
Still later development:	child's *covert* or inner speech assumes a regulatory role

Learning in school

Many studies have been done, both by observation and interview, to try to discover just what makes a good schoolteacher, or to discern under what classroom conditions children learn best. The ORACLE project will be familiar to British primary teachers as an intensive study of children and their teachers. The reports of the work (Galton and Simon, 1980; Galton, Simon and Cross, 1980; Galton and Willcocks, 1983) offer no simple answers, no blueprints for the perfect teacher, but the findings give clear indications of underlying factors which are consistent with the argument advanced in this book.

For example, six types or categories of teacher were decided from the classroom observation data: group instructors, class inquirers, infrequent changers, individual monitors, habitual changers and rotating changers. Each of these types is described in terms of characteristic behaviour, and also in terms of the commonly observed characteristics of the pupils in their classes. Thus 'class enquirers' are described as follows:

> Highly organized teachers who use class teaching for 31 per cent of the time. They are clear and lucid when explaining the work, saving a lot of time for questions and – this style's speciality – statements of ideas. Children then work individually, with the teacher helping and questioning them one-to-one. Half the class enquirers were over 40, and two-to-one were men. The majority of children in their classes are 'solitary workers', avoiding much personal contact with the teacher or other children. Their pupils made most progress of any style on maths and language tests, but significantly less progress on reading than some others. They were good at posing questions, less good at mapping and block graphs, and low on originality. (Galton and Simon, 1980)

Other categories are similarly described. 'Group instructors' tend to be 'good at listening and acquiring information from tapes and pictures'; the pupils of 'individual monitors' 'made good progress on reading but came out worst in progress on maths . . . and produced the most original drawings of all'; and so on. 'In summary,' they write:

> The successful teachers all engage in above-average levels of interaction with the pupils. They appear to devote considerable effort to ensuring that the routine activities proceed smoothly; they engage in high levels of task statements and questions, and provide regular feedback. At the same time, they also encourage the children to work by themselves towards solutions to problems. . . They manage to avoid the need to provide children continually with instructions on how to carry out the

set tasks. This comes about either because they prefer pupils to find out for themselves or because their initial instructions are so clear. These teachers, while using different organizational strategies, nevertheless have in common that they interact with the pupils more frequently than teachers using the less successful styles. Increased levels in the above kinds of teacher and pupil contact appear to be an important determinant of pupils' progress. (Galton and Simon, 1980)

A similar study by Schallert and Kleiman (1979), in America, described the characteristics of the teaching behaviour of individuals who seemed to have most success in getting their pupils to learn effectively:

1 They tailored the message to the child's existing level of understanding;
2 They reminded children of linked ideas and topics that had already been encountered;
3 They focused attention on relevant and important facts and showed children how to lay irrelevant material aside;
4 They monitored comprehension of the task 'by means of such Socratic ploys as invidious generalisations, counter-examples and reality testing', aiming to get the children to adopt these tactics for themselves.

The first of these characteristics seems obvious, and most teachers would claim that they made the effort to do precisely this in the presentation of teaching materials and in organising children into ability groupings with appropriate levels of task difficulty. Yet studies by Anderson (1981) and Cockburn (1983) suggest that this is still one of the common causes for children's failure to respond and learn properly.

Anderson's conjecture, based on classroom observation, was that for low-achieving students a state of non-comprehension or puzzlement was the norm, not least because they were so frequently mismatched with the task in terms of the complexity of vocabulary and instructions. High achievers, on the other hand, were often better matched with their work; there were fewer occasions when they did not comprehend; and Anderson concluded that they were therefore more likely to be able to monitor those occasions and seek help.

This highlighting of unexpected misunderstanding may help further the development of metacognitive skills, which could aid in information-seeking to reduce confusion, even though formal instruction seldom is focussed on the development of such skills.

In a comparable detailed study by a research group from Lancaster University, close observations of primary classrooms led to the same conclusions about the degree of mismatch between task and ability levels. A simple summary of their findings (Cockburn, 1983) revealed that:

'(a) There was a tendency for infant teachers to give the high attainers in their class tasks which were too easy for them, but to give the low attainers tasks which were too hard:

(b) Teachers sometimes had one aim in their minds (e.g. that their pupils should write an exciting story) but asked for, and rewarded, something slightly different (e.g. long, neatly written stories);

(c) A large number of practice tasks were set in which children were asked to do exercises requiring skills that they had apparently already mastered.'

To return to the other three characteristics of the 'successful' teachers outlined by Schallert and Kleiman (see p. 51), we can see that the ploys listed resemble closely the sort of learning strategies discussed in earlier chapters. Point (2) for instance, recalls Baron's 'relatedness search' strategy mentioned in Chapter 3; (3) is not dissimilar to his 'stimulus analysis' strategy and (4) resembles Baron's 'checking' strategy which involves constant monitoring of the task in hand. In short, the 'successful' teacher tends to use learning strategies herself and demonstrates them to her pupils in her teaching method.

In fact relatively few classrooms are witness to this sort of teaching behaviour: Anderson's (1981) study in America illustrated that too often the only strategies that children develop in the classroom are ones for staying out of the teacher's eye. Anderson pointed to the pervasiveness of what he called 'seatwork' assignments where children were given reading or writing assignments to be carried out without continuous teacher supervision. Closely observing teachers and young learners engaged in these activities, Anderson was struck by the poor quality of teachers' responses at the end of assignments. Almost all remarks consisted of procedural statements or simple remarks about the correctness of answers with few comments on the purpose of the exercise, the way it had been tackled or problems encountered by the learners.

It is not uncommon to find the same lack of communication in classrooms nearer home. In our own observations in primary school classrooms, for example, a similar pattern was noted when a self-testing reading scheme was in operation. Children are encouraged to take responsibility for, and monitor their own work by checking the answers to exercises against the answer card. Scores are then noted down on the front cover of their workbook. The intention of the authors of this reading scheme is presumably to encourage teachers and pupils alike in their metacognitive habits of monitoring and diagnosis. But with the sheer pressure of numbers, the response of the teacher when shown a low total score by a pupil was often to exhort them to take more time, to stop chatting while they worked, or to pronounce even more vaguely 'I told you to do it more carefully'.

Developing learning strategies

It is too easy for the detached observer to criticise existing practice. Can constructive suggestions be offered on how appropriate learning strategies can be transferred from teacher to children? Brown and Campione (1979) suggest a 'Socratic teaching method' in which the teacher constantly questions the student's basic assumptions and premises, plays the devil's advocate and probes weak areas. The aim of the exercise, they say, is not just to get the child to know on one occasion that he is wrong or mistaken and therefore needs to re-learn and re-think, but that through this form of interrogation the teacher is *modelling* for the pupil the sort of self-questioning, diagnosing and correction strategies that most adult learners perform internally and intuitively when working on their own.

> The desired end-product is that the student will come to perform the teacher's functions for himself via self-interrogation and self-regulation.

In their eyes, the most effective teachers are those who operate in the style of the enlightened mothers described earlier in the chapter. In other words they engage in continual prompts to get children to plan and monitor their own activities but with the intention not of retaining total control for themselves but of passing it over to the children as they become ready and able to take responsibility.

Several studies report attempts to use modelling techniques deliberately in order to improve the learning behaviours of different groups of children. Meichenbaum and Goodman (1971) for instance, were interested in helping children who had been diagnosed by their teachers as over-impulsive. The authors felt that these children were missing out on the sort of self-regulating internal controls that most children develop, that some deficiency existed or that some disruption had occurred in the normal transition from other-self to self-regulation mentioned earlier in this chapter. Was it possible to remediate this problem? Meichenbaum and Goodman decided to try modelling techniques to simulate the transition. Children were taken for individual training sessions with an experimenter who modelled behaviour on various psychometric or IQ tests, then encouraged the child to do the same, first verbally externalising the procedures, then internalising them. The authors compare the procedure to that in which an adult might learn to drive a car:

> One can imagine a similar training sequence in the learning of a new motor skill such as driving a car. Initially the driver actively goes through a mental checklist, sometimes aloud, which includes verbal rehearsal, self-guidance, and sometimes appropriate self-reinforcement. . . Only with repetition does the sequence become automatic and the cognitions become shortcircuited. . .

At the end of the experiment Meichenbaum and Goodman felt that they had achieved particular success in transforming children's behaviour by this demonstration modelling of alternative strategies, and felt that it was a method which would repay far wider use – especially with what they called the 'culturally deprived' child with something of a language deficit, the sort of child who 'does not spontaneously use language to direct his problem-solving behaviour, especially when specific demands to do so are removed'.

Light (1983) reports another study by Heber which set out specifically to compare the effectiveness of different teaching methods. Three types of training method were looked at:

1 An *action* condition in which the task was carried out without any related description or relevant discussion – a sort of uncontrolled 'discovery learning', or unstructured 'learning-by-doing';
2 A *didactic* condition in which the child was supposed to learn by watching the experimenter do the task – one of the most common classroom situations;
3 A *dialogue* condition in which the child was set to do the task but was required to describe and explain his actions on the task as he did so – simulating the middle stage of the transition we have noted before.

The results, summarised briefly, were that the action and didactic conditions resulted in negligible gains but that the dialogue group made greater initial progress than the others and also sustained that progress later. The point being made here is that demonstration or didacticism by itself is not enough; that is not what we mean by 'modelling'. Modelling clearly involves the transfer of control from demonstrator to pupil through a sort of transition in which language is the most important factor.

Brown and Campione (1977) make the same point at the end of the exercise in which they attempted to teach strategies for apportioning study time. They felt that the younger children in particular had need of more simple demonstrations of strategies; little progress was made in teaching children to produce the strategies spontaneously unless the experimenter had stated and described the strategy explicitly and had attempted to get the children to do likewise by prompting.

What can we glean from all this experimental work with children that throws any light on the way we might operate in the classroom? Firstly, we are looking for a teaching method that encourages the learning of strategies in context and that emphasises the value of metacognitive insights to monitor and control those strategies. A child with a good range of strategies and the capacity to produce, control and adapt them in different contexts is a flexible and effective learner.

It is possible that a variety of teaching methods is both possible and desirable in bringing about this happy state of affairs, but one idea which seems to lie at the heart of many of the methods is 'modelling', described originally from naturalistic studies of mothers and children.

Modelling seems to have a variety of characteristics which make it an effective mode of transferring knowledge and skills, but the two principal features which we might pick out here are:

1 That it represents a transitional process where control of learning is moved from teacher to learners, leaving the 'weaned' learner with responsibility for his own thinking;
2 That it consists of words and actions in some ill-defined mix that is difficult to disentangle.

Summary

This chapter considers how it might be possible to improve the level and character of children's metacognitive understanding and their use of strategies to control their learning.

Some parents are able to affect in a beneficial way the level of their children's awareness and the pattern of their learning by the way they interact with them. It is not clear whether it is what parents say or what parents do that makes the difference, but naturalistic studies of behaviour can give some guidelines as to how we might structure our own teaching patterns in the classroom.

Children are often expected to learn in a situation of competition or conflict, either with their peers or their teacher or simply with the task materials. There may be a value in this approach for children who are able to resolve this challenge in clearer insights into the nature of the problem and better understanding of their own methods of working. However, not all children are able to learn profitably in this way. The danger is that some children's puzzlement is a basis not for new learning but for opting out of the challenge.

Can we provide a more constructive model for teaching based on naturalistic studies? Modelling has been suggested as one way of developing metacognitive insights in children and of introducing them to strategies which give them control over their own learning. Between parents and children this takes place over a period of time as the child is slowly weaned to self-control. The next chapter explores how this notion of modelling could be adapted to fit the classroom and then goes on to explore alternative methods for the teacher.

6

In the Classroom: Teaching Approaches

Children – even very young children – have a considerable amount of knowledge and insight into their own cognitive process. The problem is that they don't use those insights rationally or productively when faced with a task. That is the crux of the ideas presented in earlier chapters.

Observations like those made by Waters (1982) show that as children pass through adolescence some of them at least develop the ability to harness their metacognitive knowledge and use it to operate and develop new strategies for learning.

This suggests a number of possible scenarios for teachers and learners. In the first it is assumed that strategies will emerge spontaneously in or after adolescence so that there is little point in doing anything more than teach the 'basic skills' to primary pupils. In an enlightened variant of this first scenario, teachers could still assume that natural strategy use will not occur until adolescence has been reached, but they could feel that their role was to prepare the ground – not just by teaching basic numeracy and literacy skills, but also by encouraging metacognitive awareness and the development of metacognitive knowledge, perhaps in much the same way as suggested by Flavell in 1981:

. . .We could consider teaching children to become aware of. . . their communicative goals. . . Such heightened awareness could help them choose likely means to these goals, evaluate the effectiveness of these means, and generally monitor their progress in the communicative endeavour.
. . .Try consciousness raising and training in introspection. Engage children in cognitive enterprises that should produce specificable metacognitive ideas and feelings. Try to get them to attend to these ideas and feelings.

. . .In the specific case of oral communication monitoring, get speakers and listeners to keep exchanging roles. Do this to show children how easy and familiar information can feel when you are the knowledgeable speaker and how hard and unfamiliar it can feel when you are the unknowledgeable listener. . . In short, try to stimulate conscious thoughts and feelings about speakers, messages and listeners using any methods that seem promising.

A quite different approach would be to try to shortcircuit this slow and by no means inevitable process by directly teaching or encouraging strategies in the developmentally young. Children often have the capacity for this sort of action, as we have already seen. How can they be trained to perceive cognitive goals in such a way that their metacognitive knowledge and experiences are triggered into use? That is the question that we discuss in this chapter by looking at a number of very different teaching approaches. Not all of them indulge in the same vocabulary as we have been using, and many make strange bedfellows, but it is hoped that the range of illustrations will offer some suggestions across the curriculum for the integration of ideas about metacognition and learning strategies into normal classroom procedures.

Children writing

It has been claimed that writing is one of the most powerful tools in learning. Competent, writers, it is said, can use their penned words and phrases to explore their own thoughts and develop their ideas further. How few of our school population, one wonders, ever reach this happy state where writing is a facilitator rather than an inhibitor of thought? Perhaps our teaching methods could do more in the way of offering writing to pupils as a tool for thinking and learning.

If there is any doubt of the need for a change in emphasis in the teaching of writing, one has only to refer to Spencer's (1983) survey of writing exercises across the curriculum of Scotland's secondary schools. After studying huge quantities of written output from the sample schools, Spencer found that only a quarter of the exercises set in class encouraged any form of continuous writing. Surveys of teachers showed that they were aware of the relationships between writing and learning, but that when it came to the crunch they tended to use written exercises simply as means of storing information, to reinforce memorisation or to allow the teacher to assess a pupil's understanding. Neither teachers nor pupils showed much insight into how to cope with the sorts of problems met in the *process* of writing.

It could be argued that primary schools no longer place the same heavy emphasis on storing and testing information, but it is still doubtful whether there is generally any clearer idea on how to cope with these problems encountered during the process of writing. A number of conflicting schools of thought dominate the teaching of writing and determine the sorts of activities that go on in our primary classrooms. Traditional methods characterise writing as the 'sum of separately taught sub-skills' (Spencer, 1983), and our schools are full of books containing exercises on grammar, punctuation, the topic sentence and so on. A more recent trend is what Spencer labels 'writing as the expression of personal meaning'. This essentially English movement (led by James Britton) would seem in theory to go some way towards improving the metacognitive awareness of children. The main implications of Britton's work for teachers (according to Spencer) are that 'teachers should concentrate attention on pupils' motivation to write, their perception of what they are writing for, their relationship with the reader, their own grasp of what they want to say, and their *own* language.'

A different and more specific approach to writing has been developed in Ontario at the Institute for Studies in Education. Two principal authors, Marlene Scardamalia and Carl Bereiter, have put forward the theory of 'writing as the command of strategies and techniques' (Spencer, 1983). Often running directly counter to the theories of Britton and the 'London School', the Ontario group have focused attention on the frustrations and inhibitions that the writing process presents for many young writers. A young writer's ideas are not communicated adequately because of the interferences met by the structural demands of the writing process. Experienced writers to not produce writing as a single act, but work systematically through a series of operations including planning, organising, producing text, re-reading, revising and proof-reading. These operations may occur simultaneously and may even be performed unconsciously. However, young students may find, in Spencer's words, that they 'cannot handle all these activities at once, probably do not realise the need for each of them, and have no strategies for carrying them out separately to make the demands of the task easier'. If this is so, simply encouraging pupils to write merely perpetuates the overload on their processing capacities, and they never get the chance to make automatic many of the skills involved, as mature writers have done. In other words, the inexperienced writer is in the classic state of non-comprehension that we identified in John Holt's pupils in an earlier chapter. He probably does not know what he does not know, and has little anchor on a solution to the problems that crop up during writing.

The solution Bereiter and Scardamalia offer is a training in general strategies of writing in the hope that these will become automatic and thus reduce the processing load on the young writer. Stated like this, one might be forgiven for wondering how the Ontario work differs from the much-denigrated traditionalism of skills taught in sequence and out of context. However, a quick glance at some of the classroom ideas suggested by the group (see Bereiter and Anderson, 1975 and Scardamalia *et al.*, 1981) shows the difference. Spencer summarises:

> This work is often in game form, involving collaboration among pupils to evaluate whether intentions have been achieved and to discuss how they might have been. As well as constantly reinforcing the idea of making choices to achieve effects, this work is designed to direct attention to parts of the process of writing which are normally unconscious. The aim is to teach the pupils to become aware of how they think. . .

Scardamalia's book (1981) looks at eight major problems that the writer confronts: coping with various kinds of writing (genres), planning, topic development, language, style, coherence, evaluation and revision. For each, a series of tasks or exercises or games is suggested. For example, a teacher wanted to encourage students to evaluate their own written work objectively might turn to a game called 'Who Wrote It?' After a writing exercise, students work in pairs. One of the compositions written by the pair is chosen for evaluation, but both students write a critique. The goal is to write both evaluations in such a way that other class members can't tell which one was written by the author of the composition. Such a task seems absurdly simple, yet it requires the students to step outside themselves to consider what kinds of things their partner might say. They must balance their enthusiasms or criticisms, must be careful not to appeal to private knowledge and must consider their partner's writing style. The activity must not stop there however. The class members are asked to judge who has written the evaluations and must give reasons for their conclusions. In doing so, a student might learn that he is characterised by others as overly pedantic or slapdash or too general and so on. With a repetition of the game on another occasion the students may now have a heightened awareness of their style and their personal foibles and will be able to react accordingly.

Scardamalia and Bereiter see their suggestions as distinct from the holistic approach, which emphasises the unity and meaningfulness of the whole act of composing, and the sub-skills approach. They call their own approach 'cognitive' and state (1981):

A cognitive approach is based on an effort to understand the mental processes that go in writing, and to modify those mental processes so as to enhance overall writing ability.

This concern with the *process* of writing characterises another set of ideas from America presented by Donald Graves (1983). Scardamalia's and Bereiter's technique relies on the teacher to identify strategies which are then presented to the student in game form. Students are encouraged to explore their own cognitions, but the whole set of activities is quite structured. Graves's approach represents a far less formalised technique of modelling of strategies.

In Chapter 5 we explored the idea that modelling was perhaps the most natural way to teach strategies to the young. By modelling we imply more than a mere show-and-copy procedure like that employed commonly in classrooms. Instead, modelling represents an attempt to foster a transition for the child from control and direction by others to self-regulation. A common means of achieving this transition is by verbalisation which starts off as the demonstrator thinking out loud, transfers to the child thinking out loud and, one hopes, gradually becomes internalised and unconscious.

Donald Graves has refuelled the American literacy debate with some of his theoretical challenges, but his writing is also populist, easy to read and comprises a wealth of detail about classroom life which must have particular appeal for the teacher. At first sight his work may appear more teacher-centred than child-centred with its instructions on how to arrange the classroom furniture, what materials to use, what time to allow for activities and so on. Myra Barrs (1983) points out the danger of this approach developing into a recipe book for the profession, noticing that 'the very chapter-headings (in Graves's latest book) are a check-list of teaching behaviours: "Help Children Choose Topics"; "Write with the Children"; "Publish Writing in the Classroom"; "Surround the Children with Literature".'

However, despite this, Graves's main interest is in putting children into a situation where they can 'take ownership and control at the point of knowing their subject'. In this aim and in the reflective methods that he suggests for encouraging children to recognise and make use of their own cognitive strengths and weaknesses, Graves's work is truly child-centred.

The teaching techniques advocated by Graves encourage metacognitive activities both before and after writing tasks. In the preliminary stage, teachers can use a modelling approach to demonstrate how to start to tackle a task. For instance, any of the three following methods might be appropriate:

1 The teacher sits down and writes when the children do. (The

children are not allowed to disturb the teacher as she composes.)
2 The teacher composes on to large sheets of paper so that the children can see her as she writes.
3 The teacher uses an overhead projector to write, giving a commentary as she proceeds.

The objective enshrined within any of these methods is 'to make explicit what children ordinarily can't see: how words go down on paper, and the thoughts that go with the decisions made in the writing'. Hence the teacher's verbal comments must consist of much more than simple procedural instructions. The teacher must have enough conscious awareness of his or her own cognitive processes so that the children can see, for instance, how the teacher responds emotionally and intellectually to the task set, how she establishes a suitable set of working conditions for herself, how she marshals information or searches her memory for related facts, how she copes with distractions, the stress of time limits and so on.

Graves notes that it is obviously not enough to do this once and expect children to learn anything from the experience. Children will take what they need at the time from any such demonstration, and so this method of teaching must become a common part of the teacher's repertoire.

The stress in this method, it should be noted, is that *general* strategies for learning are modelled *in context*. Graves does not see a great deal of value in setting up such an episode in order to teach a specific skill:

Children select skills in modelling more easily because they are shown within the context of natural predicaments. . . The teacher does not use modelling to beat the child over the head with a new skill. Rather, the teacher uses the modelling to confirm the commonality of all writers, as well as to confirm new approaches by the child in the writing process.

Once the writing task is under way, Graves suggests a set of activities to encourage yet more of the strategies for learning we have noted before. He suggests that 'post-mortem' activities should include a 'writing conference' or 'publishing conference' where work is reviewed, alterations made or suggestions produced for re-drafting. Finally the child is encouraged towards developing an assessment or judgment about the quality of his own work. Teachers themselves would need to decide what form these 'conferences' should take; pupils familiar with the procedure might be able to operate in groups without teacher guidance, but a first step might be to hold conference sessions in pairs or individually, with the teacher present to ask questions, lead into arguments and so on.

Many teachers already identify the need for re-drafting and revision work with children; some have made the effort to introduce it as a regular classroom procedure. The need, however, is to avoid what Graves trenchantly labels as the popular understanding of revision – 'Put a good manicure on the corpse'. Post-activity reflection must encourage children not just to dwell on the need for improved punctuation, corrected spellings and neater presentation (though this may be part of the exercise), but must also strive in a very real way to make the children responsible for quality judgments about the end-product and about the working methods which produced it.

Graves's book contains many examples of model conferences. A typical one is the following dialogue held between one child and her teacher while the girl was still working on her writing task:

'Now, how are things coming, Audrey?'
'Not too bad. I started by telling what happened when the lawnmower ran over the bees. It's kind of a poor beginning.'
'That's all right Audrey. You can change it later if you like. Sometimes in the first draft it's best just to write and tell it as it happened. Later you might want to start the lead at a more interesting part and work back from there.'

Myra Barr's critique of Graves notes that very little mention is made of children's fictional writing (the emphasis is on report-writing and personal narratives), but there is no doubt that the techniques suggested are easily adapted. Observations in the case of our own research showed one young primary school teacher intuitively using the same methods as Graves in teaching her class of ten-year-olds to write poetry. The class had been on a visit to the seashore and she chose this as a theme for a poem which she attempted to compose on the blackboard, expressing her thoughts about the theme, her nervousness at getting started, her pattern of choices and decisions about words. She created lines, stood back and reviewed them, deleted them and composed again. One must beware of a 'born again' enthusiasm for this sort of teaching approach (see Barr's comments), but it is certain that the class benefited from seeing this modelling process, for they not only set about their task with an enthusiasm and drive not normally associated with poetry-writing, but they were subsequently capable of a high degree of constructive self-appraisal and criticism.

Gibbs (1977) is only one of many who have seen this self-appraisal as the start of the real learning-to-learn experience:

Such an experience of self-discovered learning should encourage in the student a habit of examining and questioning his own studying, and a continuing process of change and development.

Where writing skills are taught in a formal or structured way they can be at best peripheral to the student's own experience of the writing process, and at worst threatening to a student lacking in self-confidence in his own ability to bend the 'rules' to suit himself. The hope is that sensitive modelling by the teacher can introduce children to broad strategies of learning and coping in contexts or situations which have real meaning for them.

In summary, these cognitivist approaches to writing are characterised by a concern with the processes of writing. They emphasise the development of broad strategies for writing and learning and are concerned with getting learners to assess their own reactions to task and context, to explore their personal strengths and weaknesses and to use these insights to improve performance. In this section we have looked mainly at two of the suggested alternative ways of encouraging children to develop these insights, namely, through strategy training (in a game situation) and through modelling and the conference-drafting approach.

Children Reading

Like writing, reading has often been seen as the sum of a number of teachable sub-skills like word-recognition, interpretation of metaphor and so on. The problem is that it is obvious that there is more to reading than the sequential processing of individual words. Reading, as Lunzer and Dolan (1979) have pointed out, is really a two-part process where:

1 The reader must establish what the writer has said (from the linguistic form of the text);
2 He or she must follow what the writer meant.

Attempts to teach putative sub-skills in reading often result in an improvement in the first, but not in the second part of the reading process. In other words children appear to have become more competent readers but their comprehension of the text remains poor and this situation must not only make their current reading experiences the poorer, but must in the long term, impose a threshold on their technical reading competence.

Technical competence is obviously an important part of *learning to read*. Unless word recognition is automated up to some minimal level, other processes important to comprehension cannot proceed because too much time or attentional capacity is used up in word recognition, as Resnick points out (1981). But what of comprehension, of the idea of *reading to learn*?

Lunzer and Dolan (1979) feel that one of the most important differences between good and bad readers (in terms of their comprehension) is the greater pertinacity of the former.

> Good readers are more willing to persist in the search after meaning even when the going gets tough. They are more aware that decoding is not enough. To that extent their reading is more purposive. They tend to ask questions ahead of what they read, anticipating what they may expect to find.

In other words, good readers are not necessarily characterised by their possession of technical skills (though this may be the case) but by their possession of a range of strategies for attacking a text and by a degree of awareness of their own reading habits and the demands of the task.

How can teachers encourage children to develop these strategic reading skills and to use them flexibly? The answer seems to lie in a number of different areas.

Firstly, teachers themselves need to be aware of how their *own* reading strategies alter when different elements of the context are manipulated. Most of us possess this form of metacognitive knowledge intuitively. We know that the readability of a text, its structure and its familiarity of content or frame of reference will all determine the ease with which we read and comprehend, and we can vary our reading strategies accordingly. A difficult piece with a number of new or technical words may cause us consciously to double-read passages if we are intent on finding meaning. We may be aware of our tendency to fasten on and remember anecdotes at the expense of the less vivid passages and may have to discipline our concentration accordingly.

Despite the fact that most teachers know this much about themselves, it is a factor that is rarely transmitted in their methods for teaching children to read. Research literature suggests a number of ways in which greater emphasis could be laid in the classrooms on nurturing learning strategies in reading.

Perhaps one of the greatest influences on the way we read is our knowledge of reading purpose. People told to read a passage in the knowledge that they will have to write a lucid summary at the end, for instance, read for comprehension much more efficiently than people told to read the passage in order to answer a set of questions. What do we know then about the sorts of reading purposes that are placed in front of our school children?

Lunzer and Dolan (1979) note that reading in schools is rarely continuous, and is often called for in short bursts. Reading usually occurs in conjunction with a follow-up exercise in writing, so that pupils are almost always reading in order to find out what to write rather than reading in order to learn.

Durkin (1979) found much the same situation when she surveyed American elementary classrooms. Her research concentrated on the classrooms of ten-year-olds, because there she believed it most likely that the switch from learning to read to reading to learn would be taking place. Three researchers operating a coding system found, however, that at this stage, in social studies periods, for example, only 1 per cent of all time went on comprehension instruction. Reading was taking place, or course, but the emphasis was on the coverage of 'facts'. Poor readers were expected to gather from round-robin reading of books by better readers or from films and filmstrips those facts that they couldn't muster from their own reading. Good readers were not being challenged because too often the type of work and the goals set were undifferentiated; social studies was a time for whole class work.

Gerald Duffy (1982) comes to the defence of teachers condemned by these findings, though without condoning the situation:

> Recently . . . researchers have studied real teachers teaching reading to real children in real classrooms. The result has been the discovery that classroom reading instruction is not a one-dimensional 'black-box' phenomenon. Instead, it is much more reminiscent of the old saying: 'When you are up to your ass in alligators, it's difficult to remember that your original objective was to drain the swamp.'

The alligators, in this case, consist of the limits to teacher's freedom imposed by school policy, curricular recommendations, resource shortages, staffing problems, parental demands and so on. Reading to learn may be a noble ambition, but it is often sacrificed in favour of – for instance – commercial reading schemes, which come ready prepared and give pupils and parents as well as teachers at least a spurious sense of progress being made. Duffy notes that interviews with teachers indicate that many of them feel these schemes are quite satisfactory, but in fact almost the only thing being taught by these commercial materials are the skills of 'decoding'. They contain little reading for enjoyment and instructing children in 'how to read' is virtually non-existent.

A great deal more attention probably needs to be paid to establishing clear and worthwhile purposes for reading. What else can teachers do to encourage all young readers to use effective and flexible strategies to reach those goals? Duffy (1982) suggests that it is more than just a question of providing the right sorts of reading materials; something far more positive is required from the teacher.

He comments:

> In sum, there is evidence to suggest that effective reading instruction is more than opportunity to learn; that teachers can do more than take pupils through instructional materials. Instead they should identify the algorithmic 'secrets' used by successful readers and set out to make these 'secrets' explicit for children so that they can 'make sense' of the reading process.

These 'algorithmic secrets' are no more and no less than learning strategies. Can these be taught directly? Certainly a large number of schemes exist which purport to train strategies for reading.

A straightforward example of this sort of procedure is the well-known SQ3R reading method advocated by Robinson (1946) where routines for reading text thoroughly and with comprehension are first taught, and then assembled into a strategy 'run' which the learner is supposed to check through each time he encounters this particular type of task.

A more modern version is Dansereau's (1978) MURDER acronym, where each of the capital letters signifies one in a sequence of strategies for reading. Dansereau is keen to point out that his sequence consists not just of the techniques involved in actually processing the text (he calls these primary strategies) but also of secondary or support strategies which the learner uses 'to maintain a suitable cognitive climate'. A MURDER sequence for tackling a reading comprehension-retention problem would thus look like this:

*M*ood – setting the mood for study
*U*nderstanding – reading for understanding (marking important and difficult ideas)
*R*ecalling material without referring to the text
*D*igesting material
*E*xpanding knowledge by self-inquiry
*R*eviewing mistakes (learning from tests)

The four basic steps in the middle (understand, recall, digest and expand) are not unlike Robinson's SQ3R and its derivatives, but two main differences exist. The first we have already noted; namely that these 'processing' strategies are embedded within a framework that causes the learner to look at himself and his cognitive characteristics, considering the conditions necessary for him to study well in the first place, and finally causing him to reflect on what he has learned. The second way in which Dansereau's scheme differs from Robinson's is that the former finds it possible to dissect these broad cognitive monitoring strategies into specific and instructable techniques. Thus instead of being told simply to 'read for understanding', children are offered a variety of tools which might help them towards that goal. At the 'recall' stage for example children are shown how to represent or transform the knowledge they have gleaned from the piece in a variety of ways such as paraphrase-imagery, networking and the analysis of key ideas.

The detailed explanation of techniques takes us back to Chapter 2 and the traditional study skills approach, and we are perhaps more interested here in what Dansereau calls the support strategies. He characterises them in hierarchial fashion thus:

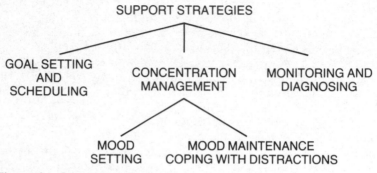

Figure 3 *Support strategies*

His suggestions for training these support strategies borrow greatly from systematic desensitisation methods, rational behaviour therapy and therapies based on positive self-talk. The triggers for the student to use these techniques once again lie in the MURDER acronym.

How useful are these ideas of Dansereau's? His own research threw up mixed results, the scheme benefiting low ability students more than high ability ones and offering good results in terms of understanding of main ideas but not necessarily recall of details.

One advantage of the scheme is that it offers a framework within which to teach specific study skills yet it is also a framework which puts emphasis on broad problem-tackling strategies. The scheme was obviously designed for fairly mature students and also best suits a syllabus with a heavy emphasis on reading, recall and essay testing. The main question that remains is whether the routine of working through the acronym is sufficient in itself to trigger off worthwhile monitoring and planning strategies, and whether any remnants of this strategic approach are transferred by the student to contexts outside the straightforward demands of the classroom. Lunzer and Dolan (1979) felt that the chief value of schemes such as these was in terms of consciousness-raising and in instilling a greater purposiveness in the reader. They asked whether there weren't less elaborate ways of achieving the same effect, a sentiment probably shared by the majority of classroom teachers.

Perhaps the simplest and probably the most effective way of inducing children to develop a keener awareness of how strategies are used to tackle reading tasks is to discuss what goes on in preparing, carrying out and reviewing a reading task. Graves's writing conference model could be adapted to allow teachers to demonstrate or model for their pupils how a reading task is approached, dissected, carried out and monitored. Too, often children are left on their own with instructions about what to read, but no guidance on *how* to read. Lunzer and Dolan feel that the trend in the last ten years or so towards mixed ability group work and the encouragement of project work in the primary school and in the first two years of secondary school has only tended to exacerbate this problem. Children are expected to cover a variety of reading tasks – reading instructions from a worksheet to find out what to do, reading a reference book to find information, reading a personal account which provides atmosphere, reading their own work for correction – but they are rarely provided with any discussion of the techniques and responses which will be called for.

To summarise, teachers can make a good start in developing strategies in their pupils by becoming aware of their own modes of working, their own problems and attitudes to different task types or contexts. As far an encouraging a similar self-awareness in children is concerned, research seems to offer a number of guidelines:

1 *Set clearer cognitive goals.* Establish clearly and highlight the purpose of reading tasks. Disaggregate tasks into their constituent parts. Make reading purposes more varied. Match goals with readers' abilities.
2 *Model strategies for reading for learning.* Demonstrate approaches to different types of reading. Strategies can be general, such as learning to establish concentration (see Dansereau, 1978) or specific, such as read and review techniques for coping with certain kinds of prose (see Robinson, 1946).
3 *Encourage metacognitive discussion.* Make explicit statements about task types, contexts, reader styles, learning problems and so on. Organise planning and post-mortem activities that review not just the outcomes of reading but also the process.

Learning to learn across the curriculum

Reading and writing tasks appear across the curriculum, and it is commonplace now to argue that emphasis should be placed on using these as opportunities for real learning in every subject, and not just those designated as language classes. Even in areas of the curriculum like arithmetic or mathematical studies there is room for an approach which encourages children to look at their methods of working and their strategies for tackling problems.

This latter point has been re-emphasised by John Seely Brown (1983) in an article in which he examines the impact the microcomputer could have on classrooms. Used wisely and used well this new addition to the teaching repertoire could, he claims, 'facilitate the learning and improvement of metacognitive skills'.

Brown's principal reason for stating this is his belief that the micro will allow increased opportunities for 'learning by doing':

> That the extension of learning by doing scenarios might also open up new ways for students to learn about the shortcomings of their own thinking should not, in principle, be surprising. It is only by trying to solve a problem and then stepping back and examining, or having someone else examine, the actual solution path that many metacognitive issues can be illustrated and/or diagnosed.

Mathematics is given as an example of a curricular area where the new generation of micros will allow children and teachers to identify systematic errors or bugs in computational procedures. Errors, instead of being regarded negatively as stupid mistakes, can be used to explore patterns of thinking and can be used to enhance learning. Brown gives the example of the 'Buggy Game' where children are invited to spot systematic errors made by the machine in order to give them an entry to the metacognitive skill of self-diagnosis.

Our own observations of micro-computers being used in primary schools give us cause to share Brown's optimism that the machines could be used in this way. Children in one school, embroiled in an electronic game involving the navigation of treasure ships and pirate craft were led by their headmaster into a discussion of their tactics, into thinking about how they had responded to their opponents' moves, into considering how certain aspects of their knowledge or lack of it had made them make false moves. The ostensible aim of the game was to encourage proficiency in dealing with compass directions and bearings, but these children were learning far more than that. Unfortunately, the sort of enlightened coaching given by their headmaster in thinking and learning was not seen everywhere. It remains to be seen whether the microcomputer will become a real aid in learning how to learn, or whether it will simply become an instrument for drill and practice or for keeping individuals amused and occupied, while the serious business of learning goes on elsewhere in the classroom.

A further interesting attempt to introduce metacognitive ideas into the classroom is seen in a piece of research carried out in an Australian secondary school by Baird and White (1984). Discussing strategies for learning these authors identify evaluation strategies (e.g. appraising, assessing, identifying, checking, etc.) as having the greatest potential for improving learning. They also believe, however, that some of the old strategy training programmes fail because they do not ultimately give students the responsibility for their own learning – too many learners remain limited to following instructions or protocols.

Their solution was to attempt a piece of 'action research' working with a teacher of science. They hoped to work at a method for developing metacognitive awareness in the pupils and encouraging in them a greater degree of participation and control for their own learning.

The main method chosen to assist students to increase control over their learning was to provide each student in three chosen classes with a 'Question-Asking Checklist'. This was to be used by the students during lessons when they were given a task to carry out. The questions required the student to challenge himself or herself about the nature of the topic, the details or information required, the nature of the specific task set, his personal approach to the problem and so on – all activities related to planning. Monitoring of the activity was encouraged by a further set of check questions, and final self-assessment completed the picture. The results of this self-questioning exercise were recorded in an evaluation notebook.

The results of the study were mixed. Baird and White felt that after a period students had begun without prompting to ask themselves higher-level questions concerning the tasks and their own cognitions, but that the ultimate goal of offering the students greater control over their learning was inevitably hampered by the relationship between teacher and pupils and the formal structures within which they worked.

Summary

In this chapter we have looked at some of the ways in which ideas about learning strategies and metacognition could be introduced into classroom life. A number of methods have been suggested by different authors for improving the method and flexibility with which children tackle learning tasks. The common element in all these ideas is a concern with the processes rather than the products of learning. Too often teachers are at pains to establish what they would like to see produced at the end of an exercise in material terms. Just how it is to be achieved and just what it contributes to the child's overall pattern of learning is most frequently left unsaid. We are forced to ask ourselves whether teachers themselves always know or are always honest with themselves about the goals and purposes of many of the exercises set before their classes. Duffy has pointed out for us that cognitive aims are sometimes sacrificed because of other social and practical pressures on the classroom, and any realistic appraisal of classroom life must take account of that fact. However, it would be pleasing to think that teachers might take on a long-term commitment to improving their pupils' ability to learn how to learn, and that they could find within the suggestions offered in this chapter, some methods that suited their personal teaching style and classroom situation.

The strategies which good learners need relate to planning of work, to monitoring of performance and to assessment and diagnosis on the completion of work. The main methods suggested here by which these strategies might be encouraged fall into three main categories.

Direct training methods require the teacher to determine what strategies are required and to offer students a framework within which to operate. The games suggested by Scardamalia and Bereiter (1981) are a rather unusual form of this direct training, but more conventional models are described by Robinson (1946), Dansereau (1978) and perhaps Baird and White (1984).

Modelling methods, such as that suggested by Graves (1983) perhaps offer greater possibilities for those who teach younger children.

Finally, discussion, whether formal or informal, will probably remain the teacher's foremost tool in developing metacognitive awareness in children. Children can be using any learning medium from the microcomputer to the Cuisenaire rods, and a thinking teacher can turn the occasion into an opportunity for real learning to take place by encouraging them to speculate on their own cognition, to examine their strategies for tackling tasks and to reflect on their own performance.

7

Working with Children and Teachers

The ideas outlined in previous chapters provided the basis for our programme of collaborative efforts with teachers and pupils over a period of two years and more. The aim was to translate general principles into practical terms and procedures which can readily be understood and applied by teachers and pupils in their regular school work. Two complementary approaches were tried: focusing teachers' attention on the strategies involved in tackling classroom tasks, and encouraging in children a greater responsibility for a clearer awareness of their own approaches to learning. We shall not attempt to present a detailed research report of all the exploratory trials but instead shall provide short extracts from some of the materials which we used.

Setting the classroom trials in context

The initial idea, at the start of the collaborative work in schools, arose from a desire to see whether the results from studies of college students' approach to learning (Entwistle, 1981) had any validity with a younger age group. The reasons for trying out the ideas with quite young children were summarised in a note of one of our meetings with a curriculum working group:

> There is evidence that by the age of nine children have a store of metacognitive knowledge about how to cope with learning tasks, but it is an unreflective knowledge, and it is generally inadequately applied in transfer situations.
>
> Action is intuitive. By age ten, however, most children are becoming at ease with fundamental tools, e.g. in reading and numeracy. They are moving into a stage of increasing capacity for conscious planning and direction of their own learning.

What often happens in practice is that over the years young people cobble together their own rules for handling school work. As the years pass it becomes increasingly difficult to change these rules. The battery of tactics which students bring to college is firmly established and is largely the result of chance associations of successes and failures with tactics employed at various points in their earlier learning histories.

Much of the work in the last two years of primary school at present is task directed, and though the ability to achieve success in set learning tasks is important, it does not of itself generalise to other learning tasks. Specific task-directed work does not nurture autonomous learning. Skill practice in abstraction from real contexts, and without self-monitoring, does not lead to flexibility and transfer.

In the first two years of secondary school at present, there is a massive amount of directed learning. Competence is narrowly defined in specific curriculum areas; there is little integration of skills or attention to high-level strategies; and the curriculum is overcrowded. These are features which tend to inhibit generalisation of learning.

. . .Before age ten, conscious self-direction of learning is relatively rare; by fourteen, many pupils can plan action consciously. Ten to fourteen are years of opportunity. Too often they are wasted years.

This summary of the argument so far can be put beside three beliefs which we set down as general hypotheses:

1 Most people are capable of better learning than they currently demonstrate.
2 Better learning depends on the development of learning strategies.
3 The key to this development is awareness and monitoring of one's own mental processes.

The immediate problem was how to translate these ideas into classroom processes. Against these lofty ideals, the practical work which we were able to do inevitably seems limited. The ideas are difficult in themselves; working with young children possibly makes them harder still to translate into practice. However, between the ages of ten and fourteen children are very alert to new modes of behaviour, and it seemed to us that these are the years when their patterns of adult behaviour are being established.

Initially we planned to use observation and interviews to try to detect whether the children were in fact learning to learn, beginning to adopt consistent strategies, consciously or intuitively, in their handling of classroom work. The strategies we noted were narrowly specific within prescribed classroom tasks: a method for each kind of number problem, once the nature of the problem had been established – and all the problems were presented in batches, all of the same kind; a method for exercises involving reading and answering questions; a set procedure for project work, and so on. These strategies were applied intuitively rather than consciously; and they were determined largely by the teachers, either through procedures taught explicitly or through approaches which were implicit in the teachers' presentation of tasks for the children. Consequently, we began to consider whether we could persuade teachers of the need to teach generalisable strategies and influence the children's learning in this more direct way. Later, our interest focused more precisely on encouraging children to develop and articulate their own strategies. Discussion, planning, monitoring their own progress, redrafting, checking, reflection and analysis of their successes and difficulties and errors, were the means to achieve this, with the help and guidance of their teachers. Thus our ideas shifted as a result of classroom trials, as the children and their teachers helped to give new and more hopeful directions towards a solution.

A set of exemplars

One technique which we used (in the later stages of the collaboration) was to give our helping teachers a folder of practical examples. In an introductory note, we wrote:

> The folder comes to you incomplete. Our aim is to add sections as the weeks progress, in response to your suggestions. A tentative list of sections follows this foreword, but we hope that you will guide us on the type of material you would like to see included.

The aim was not to inflict yet another rule book on teachers and children, but to encourage teachers to work out their own procedures within a framework which was outlined at the beginning of the folder. Extracts from a version for primary school teachers (amended in the light of trails) will perhaps convey the flavour of the contents.

> How can we best teach children to 'learn how to learn'? One approach can be seen in the proliferation of study skills manuals in recent years. Most of these seem to have little to offer the teacher of primary school children. They are often aimed at teaching children to play the secondary school system – how to

pass exams, listen to lectures and so on – and moreover they are based on morsels of 'good advice' passed down through the generations but rarely tested against the reality of the classroom.

We hope that training for learning in the primary school can be carried out in a much more enlightened way, building study skills into the normal work of the classroom across the whole curriculum. In particular, we are interested in trying an approach based on two main ideas:

(i)   teaching not only subject or task-specific skills, but also the 'superordinate' skills or strategies that encourage children to integrate skills in a way that will encourage transfer from task to task;
(ii) training children to develop an awareness of how they may control and monitor the learning process.

Both of these ideas deserve a little more explanation and discussion.

Training skills and strategies

There has already been a considerable amount of attention paid to 'skills' in the primary sphere. Some schools already have a curricular grid of skills for teachers' guidance in drawing up their syllabuses and class teaching plans. Publishers' catalogues are full of books containing reading or writing schemes devised to practise or extend specific skills.

However, the great problem in skills training has always been this: how can we get children to move from the stages where they use skills, but only on teacher's command or instructions, to the stage where, faced with a problem, children can pull together a number of skills from their repertoire to produce a spontaneous strategy for its solution?

Children are often taught a variety of skills during their last two years in primary school, including how to use a reference book index, how to skim-read, how to write reports and so on. However, if these same skill-trained children were let loose on project work, the chances are that these skills would fly out of the window as they set to copying, pasting and keeping very busy with whatever apsect of the topic took their fancy.

These children have the specific skills for project work, but they have not been taught the main strategy, or tactic, or superordinate skill for tackling project work – namely that it is important to set up a question or hypothesis, and then to gear

one's information-gathering, reading and writing activities
towards this goal.

Training control and monitoring of learning

All children need to be encouraged to reflect on the learning
process rather than concentrate on the finished product. This
involves discussing and analysing with the teacher. . .
  – what the goals of the exercise are and how they relate to
    previous work . . .   (*preparation*)
  – what the best means of achieving those goals are; what
    skills and information are necessary. . .   (*planning*)
  – what quality is the final piece of work produced; what did
    each child learn from it; what aspects of it could be used
    again. . .   (*reflection*)
The chief tool of the teacher in carrying out a training on these
lines is obviously her ability to discuss learning with the class,
though she might be able to incorporate ideas like self-
questioning exercises or checklists as shown in some of our
case-study material.

The broad aim is to encourage children to take a more active
part in assessing their own learning rather than waiting passively
for instructions or procedures. In other words, children are given
back the responsibility for their own learning.

Our two main ideas are not really separable. We think that
learning to learn can best be accomplished by direct training in a
variety of levels of skills and strategies, accompanied by an effort
on the part of the teacher to encourage a degree of self-
awareness and self-monitoring of learning performance in the
child.

We hope that the following sections will clarify these ideas by
presenting them in the context of classroom situations familar to
all primary teachers.

A list of topics followed:

1 Using broadcast materials
2 Planning project work or individual research topics
3 A fieldwork visit or trip
4 Using games and simulations
5 Setting homework
6 Using the school computer
7 An imaginative writing exercise
8 Reading and comprehension
9 Children's reports and essays

10 Teaching mathematics
11 Preparing worksheets
12 Finding information

'Using broadcast materials' was put first because most teachers are familiar with the application of these principles in the use of schools broadcasts. Perhaps this was a mistake, because it prompted the response, 'We are doing this already: there is nothing new here.' The conventional advice on preparing and reflection (or 'post-mortem', as we called it in our first draft) was followed by three checklists as a guide to the teacher. The checklist on planning, for example, invited the teacher to check the 'goals' or purposes she had in mind in using the material, and to relate these goals to 'skills and tactics' (concentration, memory, discrimination, note-taking). Each checklist was accompanied by a selection of 'appropriate' activities for follow-up, as described by primary school teachers from their own experience. For example, included under 'Using broadcast materials' (though it could have gone with any of several topics) was the following example from the teacher's notes:

> It's always been school policy here to give two marks or comments on kid's work – for presentation and for effort. I thought I'd extend the idea by separating the two completely just for a term. No piece of work was handed in without an account of how it had been done, usually just a paragraph (though they also kept a diary when we did our project). The finished piece of work got one mark and the 'process' account got the other. . .

Finally, for each of the topics, a case study was included, to illustrate how the topic could be developed in the school context.

The material for 'Using games and simulations' concentrated on how to use games as a starting point for discussion on strategies – without spoiling the fun:

> Games need to be played, not talked about beforehand, so once the rules and the necessary information are clear it may be as well to get started. . .
>
> The whole impact of the game as a learning situation is lost if there is not time afterwards for reflection on what went on. Children will be keen enough to talk about their level of achievement and success in the game, but there's usually nothing in the game rules or package to extend their thinking beyond this point.
>
> For example, *Hangman* can be used as a vocabulary/spelling game. (There is a computer version: if you have access to a

computer, see if there is a *Hangman* programme.) Pupils work in pairs (or as pupil versus computer). One 'pupil thinks of a word, indicating the number of letters – – – – –, possibly giving a clue. The other says a letter: if it is in the word, it is inserted in the correct place; if not, the first forfeit is lost. Each forfeit is one part of a gallows (10 errors maximum). The 'guesser' wins if he or she completes the word before the gallows is complete.

Let the children practise this for a time (if they are not already familiar with it). Then ask them to write down instructions on 'how to win at hangman'. Discusss the answers. They will include some obvious rules:

1 Start with E, the most frequent letter;
2 Every word must have a vowel, to follow with the other vowels;
3 Follow with the most frequent consonants (which are they?);
4 With long words, there are certain sequences which appear often – standard prefixes, or endings like -ing or -ent.

Let the children produce these rules for themselves.

The unit on 'The microcomputer in the classroom' similarly emphasised discussion of strategies:

> Great play has often been made of the service we are doing to our primary schoolchildren by exposing them at an early age to the new technologies that will dominate their later lives. It is doubtful whether this is really the case if micros continue to be used in schools as they are now. An over-emphasis on game-play which requires passive responses to automated commands, the complete de-contextualisation of computer education in relation to the rest of the curriculum and a lack of training in the weaknesses of computer language and thinking compared to children's own rich experience in both are perhaps only characteristics of this early stage of computer use. As familiarity increases, teachers will have the leisure and capacity to examine how the machines might best be used to encourage and facilitate learning.
>
> Checklist A starts by suggesting a variety of ways in which microcomputers might be of use in the primary classroom. The advantages and disadvantages of different types of micro activity are explored very briefly, together with some suggestions for ways in which the opportunities to learn offered by the machine can best be capitalised.
>
> Most teachers will want to preview or run through tapes or discs themselves before unleashing them on their class. Information packs often give little indication of their content

other than a statement about the topic covered. Teachers will want to know in what ways the topic is explored, whether it necessitates prior knowledge on the part of the children or whether it can be used as a training item from scratch. An initial run-through helps the teacher to plan resources and timetable the use of the machine more realistically. The teacher will also use her experience of her own class to estimate whether the suggested age-level of the program makes it suitable for use with particular children. Checklist A continues with a straightforward list of questions that the class teacher might want to ask with regard to each program she decides to use.

Checklist B looks at a further issue, though it is not one you will want to tackle every time the micro is switched on. Planning exactly how the micro is to be used in the classroom is a subject which repays discussion in a school, not just to create a uniform policy, but to share ideas and experience. Although the two examples offered might seem to centre around organisational issues, they are important for the ways in which they affect the type of learning experience children undergo.

However long the programs themselves take it is almost always worth taking a little extra time afterwards to reflect on what has happened. Unlike in many other spheres of school activity, children are keen to talk about their success or failure, the reasons for it, the way they'd do it given another chance and so on. In addition, they are able to talk about programs, their choices and reactions in a much more perceptive way than they are able, for instance, to talk about the way they tackled a comprehension exercise. The teacher who takes the trouble to intervene at this stage not only learns for herself what further work is necessary with the children but is able to encourage them to be constructive in the way they plan and reflect on their work. Checklist C offers several suggestions for appropriate types of follow-up work that teachers might want to adapt for their own use.

Earlier trials

These examples are drawn from one of the later stages of collaboration with groups of teachers. Earlier, the approach was more exploratory, aiming to discover whether, at the late primary and early secondary stages, children do in fact use deliberate strategies in tackling their work, or whether they merely work routinely, carrying out procedures unquestioningly. (The conclusion was: yes, they *have* strategies, but they are not skilful at *using* them.) We set specific classroom tasks (reading a passage and answering questions, drawing a pie-chart, solving a number problem) and asked them to describe their method. Transcripts of recordings made during these introspective interviews were analysed for evidence of one approach or another. The method was tried with both primary and secondary pupils. It was difficult, but not impossible, to get such young children to introspect during the task or after completing it. But the main obstacle was that the interviews were lengthy procedures and had to be conducted outside the classroom, even though typical school tasks were chosen. It was clear that the peculiar situation in which we placed the children was eroding the concept of 'ecological validity', so drastically had we altered the normal class context. Even the need to verbalise as they worked has an effect (a beneficial one) on the level at which many children operated.

The use of tests designed to reveal different styles of approach (for example, a sentence verification test which claimed to differentiate between reading for meaning and superficial reading), and a questionnaire adapted from the type used by Entwistle and Wilson (1977) with students, also demonstrated the dominant influence of context. The perceived aims of the task, the audience for the product, the manner of presentation, the degree of familiarity with the task-type: these were just some of the many facets of the context that seemed to determine the way children set about learning and the strategies they used.

Results and conclusions

Which aspects of the context most clearly influenced the children's approach to their work? This question was explored in two ways: first, detailed interviews with secondary school pupils about the methods they adopted over a range of tasks; second, classroom observation in primary and secondary schools to try to identify, in an informal way, the effect of teaching method on the strategies which children adopted.

The first of these studies confirmed the belief that children used a range of approaches depending on the context in which the task was set. In many cases the strategies they used were redundant, inefficient and unsophisticated, and yet they served well to answer the sorts of questions and problems set, all of which were typical school tasks.

This impression was confirmed by the classroom observations. We had been concerned to discover what strategies the teachers were promoting. The disillusioning conclusion recorded in our working notes was that 'there seemed to be little or no emphasis on the way things are learned or tasks carried out'.

A more systematic test of this conclusion during an intensive period of classroom observation attempted to code unambiguously and simply whether teachers were modelling strategies, teaching them directly, incorporating them in classroom materials or ignoring the learning process. Follow-up interviews with a small number of children explored the children's view of the task-goal and the method used in the class work which had been observed. Before the lessons, the teachers themselves recorded their objectives, and were interviewed afterwards. The disappointing conclusion that emerged, possibly influenced by the way the inquiry was designed, was that the teachers had little notion of the sorts of strategies the children would use or need: instructions, advice and assessment usually revolved around the end-product of the task. Consequently children saw their principal goal in terms of 'doing' or 'completing' a task, and geared their strategies to that end.

An exploratory study

A group of primary and secondary school teachers agreed to work with us to see whether they could incorporate the idea of learning strategies into their normal classroom work. This was an exploratory, open-ended study: teachers reported on a diary sheet where they felt they had been able to emphasise or incorporate training of a strategy for learning into their work. As a starter, they were given various papers including exemplars on 'Drafting and checking' and 'Planning a work schedule', and one entitled 'Why not try these ideas?'

a   Discuss different types of reading with your class. Give them practice in reading for pleasure, reading to find information, scanning for points, key-words, etc. Talk to them afterwards about the *way* they read rather than what they read. Can they tell the difference?

b   Get your pupils to make a list of the things they feel they have to learn by heart in your class. You'll be surprised at the results! Sift out the odd ideas and get them to think about different ways of remembering or learning by heart. See if they can think of four or five ways of remembering in a simple task (learning spellings of new words, for example), then give them a 'learning' exercise for homework and quiz them afterwards about the way they did it. Did knowing about other people's strategies for remembering affect their performance? . . .And so on, to 'h'.

They all tried radically different approaches, from straight didactics (teaching a routine) to encouraging group discussion and exploration of individual problem-solving strategies. The papers on 'Drafting and checking' and 'Planning a work schedule' were almost wholly ignored. The 'ideas sheet' was the source used most extensively (though it had been cobbled together rapidly at the last minute as an afterthought). The diaries were well kept by some; others found them restrictive and opted to report on their activities in a less structured way. One secondary school teacher recorded:

We then looked at their ability to read for information. They had already learned that they needed to acquire new reading methods, particularly when faced with research tasks. The method acquired in primary school is long, laborious, and usually results in copying out word-for-word large pieces of admittedly relevant information.

I insisted that each pupil give evidence of having understood the task, and acquired the information by presenting the information in another form: for example, if material was found in a book it had to be presented as a talk. This meant that scan/skim reading skills were recognised as essential, that the finding and selection of words were realised by the pupils as of major importance, and that structured note-taking was felt to be highly desirable, though initially almost impossible to achieve.

We were reading instructions for making Christmas decorations, an activity that the whole class was very interested in. The instructions were fairly clear, though not entirely so. After 15 minutes' reading, most of the class announced (in various ways) that they were bored. They clearly were not: so we analysed what had been happening. They told me that they were in fact imagining each process and that this was something that they found both difficult and tiring. I, on the other hand, in common with most English teachers, had always regarded the reading of instructions as 'Transactional' and therefore easy and basic.

Instructions were factual; novels were imaginative. I had been fundamentally misjudging the difficulty of the nature of the task I had set, for to imagine in a closed context *is* far more difficult than in the free-ranging area of the novel.

The teachers were given a report on the results, with anonymity ensured:

Teacher 1 was able to try a number of approaches through the whole age range of the secondary school. He concentrated, in different exercises, on getting children to reflect on their strategy for tackling a particular task and on encouraging them to plan a new strategy for tackling a writing task. Groups were encouraged to develop drafting and revision procedures in order to improve the quality of the final product, but also to see whether a deliberate strategy for checking affected their attitude to the task. . .

Teacher 2 reported on group work in the primary school. Illustrations were given of exercises designed to encourage children who had difficulty in creative writing to compose on tape, and then use the same medium to edit and assess their own work before producing a final 'draft'. In addition the teacher reported on how group discussions with children could be used to guide them to introspect about and assess their own performance, as well as to help them formulate strategies for action. . .

Teacher 6 concentrated on using one particular area of skills, namely note-taking. This was used as the basis, however, for a very broad attempt to get children to reflect on their current modes of working. By emphasising the multi-modal nature of note-taking the teacher encouraged children to reflect upon their purposes and their goals in taking and using notes. Several different models of note-taking were presented and discussed.

The field notes (edited to remove identifiable comments) gave a more frank assessment of the outcome.

X could never really understand what we were asking her to do. . . Consequently she had a great deal of trouble producing anything on the diary sheets. . . Yet she is undoubtedly a teacher who does encourage independence of thought and action in her class. . . She has served a useful purpose in reminding us that it is possible to teach well by intuition and instinct without being able to explain one's methods and objectives clearly.

Y concentrated on one group of primary children working on maths problems. Most of her efforts seemed to be directed at getting the children to talk about the way they had tackled a set of fairly simple numerical problems. She got them to do this by talking, by writing down their steps and finally by drawing a simple set of flow diagrams.

Z did sterling work: the large number of trials he carried out is attested to by the bulk of his diary sheets. . . I enjoyed his the best, mainly I think because the emphasis in all of them is not on what he did, but rather what the children got out of the

experience. . . He was quietly critical of some of the ideas we
had suggested. . . He felt that they lacked a clear internal
consistency or theme.

Many other examples could be given to illustrate applications of the
ideas suggested. One teacher was teaching her mathematics class
how to use calculators. Following up the instructional lessons and
practice, she had the class discussing strategies for using the calculators appropriately and effectively, noting and analysing the problems which the pupils met in using them and developing the
discussion on these problems to help the pupils diagnose their own
faults. Another used modelling in demonstrating how to write a
poem, not merely explaining a procedure but discussing with the
children the choices made, the reasons for decisions, the constraints
and the intentions at each stage as the poem was created. In a
project on 'finding out' from a library, a teacher followed up the
activity by having the children explain (and consequently examine)
how they set about the task, and then discuss each other's
products in the light of the discussion. In another class, two boys
who were backward in writing, were set to compose a story on a tape
recorder, with accompanying sound and dialogue. The boys were
then set the task of deciding which parts of the tape needed editing,
whether the ending was satisfactory, which parts were especially
interesting or exciting; and in their discussion of these questions
they demonstrated an unexpected capacity for critical analysis at a
simple level.

The need for structure?

The teachers' general reaction was that something more structured
and easy to follow was needed. To quote from the field notes again:

Teachers don't mind putting in the effort to think things
through, prepare new materials, set up resources and rearrange
their syllabus. . . but the effort of doing this for every class and
every task becomes an overwhelming burden without more
specific guidelines and routines.

This was the reason why we compiled the folder of more structured
examples mentioned above. The structure was intended as a support for teachers and was provided by spelling out the applications
of the ideas to five of the twelve topics listed earlier in this chapter,
numbers 1, 2, 4, 5 and 6. The other topics were left unfinished to
indicate that the folder of examplars was not meant to be used as a
work-book, and certainly not as a recipe book. The response to the

folder was mixed. Their circulation extended beyond the co-operating group (without our knowledge or approval), and it seemed that many teachers liked them and found them stimulating. Some head teachers used them in staff development meetings as a starter for discussion. Other teachers found them irritating and unrealistic. The way they were used was that, as with other teaching resources, some parts were liked and these were extracted and used or pirated and adapted; but this pattern of use did not foster any new insights into learning to learn or alter teachers' general approach.

One difficulty at this stage of development of the idea was that the co-operating teachers were uncertain whether *they* were expected to develop strategies for teaching or whether the children were expected to develop strategies for learning. The principal aim was to develop children's learning strategies (and that was the message in the introduction to the folder); but the examples in the folder suggested teaching strategies which would encourage learning to learn, and this caused some confusion.

Another weakness was the lack of a developmental element in working out the idea. The examples and the discussion did not refer to specific ages or classes, and did not show how the teaching and learning might develop over a period of years. Some teachers seemed to interpret learning strategies as if they were skills which, like riding a bike or swimming, could be ticked off one by one as they were taught and mastered. We saw the 'possession' of learning strategies as a long-term aim. One might expect children to be reaching a degree of proficiency in adopting and applying strategies by age fourteen, but certainly not to see them fully developed by age ten. What can reasonably be expected of children at ten, twelve and fourteen remains to be explored.

Other teachers complained that this approach to learning took for granted that the children were above average and well-motivated, and that our presentation had not faced up to the problem of the slow learner, the pupil with learning difficulties or the ones with 'lowest ability'. Discussion of methods, for example, was considered to be unsuited to their classroom problems. The field notes unsympathetically comment:

> Partly this reflects their apathy and lack of imagination in
> adapting the suggested materials to their own situation.

But the issue goes deeper: it was one of the unstated ideas (deliberately not stated, for fear of claiming too much) that the slow learners in particular would benefit from this kind of teaching and experience. Much of the psychological work on metacognition was done with subjects of low ability. There is an argument for reversing the conventional assumption: not that children who lack ability are poor at learning strategies, but rather that children who lack learning strategies have poor ability.

These criticisms, however, suggested to us that in our presentation we had over-emphasised the idea of metacognition, at the expense of the broader learning strategies. The self-monitoring involved in metacognition is only one of three methods which are advocated in the previous chapters, and possibly the other two, direct teaching and modelling, deserved more emphasis. Several of the teachers who took part in the trials said that they wanted clearer guidance on what to teach and what to expect from the children. The teachers in one school in particular argued for hierarchies of skills and strategies specified in behavioural terms for each of several areas in the curriculum, but this suggestion was resisted.

The reason for hesitating to present detailed structures was that this could imprison the general principle within a set of context-specific activities. Transfer, or generalisation, was the primary aim – the application of an idea to novel situations. The way to achieve this is not to prescribe rules, but to create understanding and a change of attitude which should make the prescription of rule unnecessary. We too have to 'teach for transfer', by pointing out the transferability of strategies. This is not an excuse for avoiding the precise working out of procedures in a classroom context. An understanding of the underlying principles is essential in order to get the teachers and the children working out strategies for themselves. Anything less would fall short of the ideal of 'learning to learn'.

Summary

This chapter outlines in summary the practical work which we did over a two-year period with teachers and children, trying to translate the principles of 'learning strategies' into classroom procedures. Essentially, the aim was two-fold: to focus teachers' attention on learning strategies and to encourage in the children an awareness of their own approaches to learning.

Interrogating children (aged ten to fourteen) about their methods of learning showed that children have developed strategies intuitively but they are not skilful at using these strategies appropriately. Observation of classrooms revealed that there were relatively few occasions when attention was directed to the way things are learned or tasks carried out. The products are emphasised and the processes tend to be neglected.

Techniques to try to open up the issues for teachers included lists of suggestions, outlines of procedures, diary sheets and case studies for discussion, and a manual of exemplars. It was clear that the approach to learning which is derived from the cognitive psychology research reported earlier is not easily translated into classroom practice. It can be explained by carefully designed and structured examples; but teachers need to understand the underlying principles if they are to develop this approach constructively and flexibly.

8

Learning Strategies in the Curriculum

Up to this point, all that has been claimed is that metacognition and the learning strategies model can enlighten, inform and guide teaching and learning across the curriculum. Learners who are able to apply learning strategies flexibly and can monitor their learning processes will learn more efficiently as a result. Teachers who have grasped the idea of metacognition will be able to help their pupils and students to become better learners.

Radical change?

Can we go further than this, to suggest that these recent developments in cognitive psychology could provide the basis for radical rethinking of the curriculum? G. Brown (1984), for example, suggested that 'metacognitive theory could offer valuable contributions to the arguments about a core curriculum'. While acknowledging that subject content was one factor in deciding what should be in the core, he speculated on the possibility of basing the curriculum on 'essential metacognitive skills which improve the efficiency of the children's cognitions'. 'Improving the efficiency of cognition' translated literally into plain English means teaching people to think. Can a curriculum achieve this?

The Inspectorate Report, *Mathematics 5–11* (1979), claimed that 'mathematics trains the mind'. The Robbins Report (1963) listed as one of the four aims of higher education, 'to promote the general powers of the mind'. Psychologists have tended to challenge such assertions as being vague to the point of meaninglessness. But in recent years, they have moved nearer the idea and towards a new interpretation of 'ability'. In the field of reading, for example, Francis (1985, quoting Baron 1978 and others) shows how the paradigms of recent research in reading have shifted away from attempts to analyse 'reading ability', aiming instead to identify the component strategies involved in the process of reading. (This section of Francis's paper is headed 'From abilities to strategies'.) The difference may appear slight, but it is a significant change. Diagnosing reading difficulty as due to lack of reading ability is a piece of circular reasoning; identifying the component skills points a way to improve performance.

Applying this more generally, if ability (as demonstrated in performance) is interpreted as the product of some innate quality of mind, we are given little help in trying to improve a learner's performance. If ability is taken to be the acquisition of strategies of learning, we can perhaps do something about it– even if we may have to admit that some people seem to be better than others in learning the necessary strategies.

By learning, we can improve our performance in various activities. Is there perhaps some syllabus of studies which can improve our competence in learning? This has been the aim of American research on 'intellectual skills training', as it is usually termed. Success has been achieved with mentally handicapped children, whose competence can be improved significantly by appropriate training in procedures. But this kind of training in specific procedures is sadly limited (like some study skills programmes, which merely train pupils how to pass exams and get good grades). The use of mnemonics, for example, is a device which we can all adopt to improve specific memory, but it does not improve our general reasoning powers. Only if there is transfer – if the skills and strategies learned in one context can be applied in a new and different context – can we begin to speak of 'learning to learn'.

Sternberg's work on intellectual skills training has been mentioned in Chapter 3. Other writers have attempted to teach 'problem-solving' (see Baird, 1983, and Frederiksen, 1983, for reviews of research in this field). Rubinstein (1975), for example, offered a list of general strategies: seek a general pattern behind the detail, delay commitment, create models, transform into a different context, question premises, dredge the memory, work backwards from the stated goal, locate sub-structures, apply analogies, incubate. But these are an unrelated set of procedures, lacking a coherent theory. According to Simon (1973), the teaching of problem-solving must differentiate between well-structured problems (as are set in school arithmetic, for example) and ill-structured or fuzzy problems which we encounter in real life. If only all our problems could come ready packaged as in school texts, with relevant facts supplied and irrelevant ones excluded! A first step is to recognise that a problem exists, and then to structure it in such a way that one can begin to apply problem-solving strategies and previous knowledge to solve it. Traditional school instruction does not train us for this kind of thinking. Those who devise courses in problem-solving urge the same kind of awareness of cognitive processes which we have summarised within the concept of 'meta-cognition'.

In the context of established studies

However, it is not necessary to devise a new syllabus based on intellectual skills or problem-solving in order to apply learning strategies in the curriculum. A more practical proposal – and probably a more effective means – is to set the teaching of learning strategies firmly in the context of established classroom studies. Conventional subjects can provide a basis for teaching learning strategies, provided that subject content and subject-based skills are taught in a way which encourage transfer.

This is the recommendation of the NFER research project on study skills, quoted in Chapter 2. The teaching of study skills must not become another subject in the curriculum:

It may be better conceived as the provision of support for the study problems that students already encounter in their subject classes . . . carefully planned to augment the teaching, and learning which students already regard as important.
(Tabberer and Allman, 1983)

If there is to be generalisation and transfer, then both teachers and students must be made aware of the need to apply strategies flexibly. Tabberer and Allman refer to 'training which raises awareness' as a 'key element' in transfer.

Thus learning strategies need not run counter to the conventional structure of the curriculum. They are means to an end rather than ends in themselves.

The need for a learning strategies approach will become more pressing as schools move away from the reproductive modes of learning that have characterised study in the past. Traditional notions about learning and study skills served the needs of students within that system rather poorly; they have relatively little to offer children in an age where technological change occurs so rapidly that not only information but also narrowly defined vocational skills rapidly become redundant. School learning in the future seems likely to be characterised by a higher degree of independent, self-motivated learning, by tasks which call for thinking rather than reproduction of facts, and by the demand that results be communi-

91

cated. In all those cases the need is for broader strategies which transfer from task to task and which involve a higher level of self-monitoring than teachers have been accustomed to expect from their pupils.

A project initiated in 1981 by the Council for Educational Technology illustrates this evolution in classroom practice. The Supported Self-Study Project (Waterhouse, 1983) was designed with educational aims in mind and also to meet a need in schools where falling numbers on the roll threatened curriculum choice. Their stated aims were:

1 To help pupils develop autonomy giving them more responsibility for their studies and the opportunity to learn how to learn;
2 To help schools to respond to the special needs of individuals and minority groups, and to protect subjects and activities that may currently be at risk.

Supported self-study is the method designed to achieve this:

It is an arrangement whereby a pupil pursues a whole course of study, or part of a course, through the use of structured learning materials, with tutorial support from a teacher. It can be regarded as an alternative to class teaching or as a supplement to it. It can be organised on any scale: large enough to represent a transformation in the working philosophy of the school; or small enough to provide an enriching experience, with minimum upheaval.

A combination of practice

Those who advocate a larger role for learning strategies and meta-cognition in the curriculum usually envisage combining them with the learning of subject-matter and subject-specific skills. Resnick and Beck (1976), for example, were particularly concerned with reading instruction, but their recommendations have a general application:

1 *Teach in context*. Teaching should focus heavily on building up extensive bodies of knowledge that will help pupils to interpret new materials that they encounter. As far as reading is concerned, this means less reliance on collections of brief, unrelated reading selections in favour of extended reading and related experiences in a few areas of interest.
2 *Teach general strategies*. Teaching should encourage general

strategies of reasoning and thinking that have application across the curriculum.

3 *Teach mediational strategies.* Teach specific and explicit skills such as techniques for organising and remembering information that has been read (visual imagery, self-questioning, networking, re-grouping of information, etc.).

4 *Teach meta-comprehension.* Try to help children to become aware of learning processes and to call deliberately on their most effective strategies. Encourage children to monitor and organise their own comprehension processes.

Such a system provides a way of resolving the dilemma that faces teachers when they are told that learning is best done in context, embedded in a real or worthwhile experience, and yet it is obvious that at some points particular skills or strategies need to be picked up and emphasised.

Kirby (1984) in arguing for an educational 'mix' of teaching models also mentions this dilemma. Should one teach broad strategies such as planning and monitoring, emphasising awareness? Or should one teach a variety of more narrow task-specific skills? His conclusion was that neither of these approaches would be very successful in isolation. Broad strategies are difficult to change, demand long-term application and are difficult to attack in the absence of specific tasks or contexts. Narrow skills, on the other hand, are easy to change or to train in the short-term, but are less likely to generalise.

> The solution . . . is to combine both within a coherent
> approach. A few highly specific schemes or skills must be taught
> first to provide a basis for understanding, but some higher-level
> accomplishments must follow soon to preserve motivation.
> Basic schemes should be highly practised, so as to minimise the
> processing resources they absorb, but drill should not last long
> at any particular time. It should be alternated with higher level
> activities, which in turn make use of the lower level schemes
> just drilled.

This conclusion is reflected in the work of Bereiter and Scardamalia on teaching writing skills to young children, described in Chapter 6.

Three crucial questions are linked together. Are there generic learning strategies which cut across subject boundaries? (And surely there are.) Are most skills so embedded in context that they can only be learned in a specific context? (This also is true.) But by distinguishing 'skills' and 'strategies', we have a means of access to the third question: how do we teach for transfer? Though specific skills are embedded, the more general strategies are not; and metacognitive awareness and control are more feasible with the more complex processes in learning.

Thus in no sense are learning strategies a *substitute* for the traditional curriculum content of knowledge and subject-related skills. Some contemporary writers seem to imply that knowledge goes out of date so quickly that it is a waste of time to require children to learn knowledge: instead, let them learn how to acquire knowledge. This is an unrealistic and invalid argument. Learning to learn must be done in a real context: the best way to acquire strategies of learning is in the process of learning. But if what is learned is to be transferable to other contexts, then it must be taught in such a way as to encourage transfer. The suggestion here is that this be done both by emphasising the teaching of general strategies for learning and by encouraging the sort of self-awareness and awareness of task and context which we have labelled as metacognition.

Learning strategies in the classroom

There is no doubt that there are substantial problems in implementing these ideas in the classroom. Even teachers convinced of the merits of the notion may be restricted by their lack of training in certain techniques (like holding group discussion), may suffer from a shortage of materials that support this approach, or may feel compelled to modify it in the face of parental expectations and the demands of the syllabus.

Perhaps most daunting is the knowledge for teachers that, at the moment, they are on their own. The ideas discussed in this book do not come pre-packaged, and, although condensed, will not swell up into full-blown teaching schemes with the addition of a few spoons of water. Any teachers currently interested in the ideas must sift through the material, preparing guidelines for themselves that best match their own teaching styles, that suit their teaching aims and that will best benefit the type of children with whom they are involved. Perhaps only when the ideas become incorporated into curriculum objectives and structures and 'whole-school' policies are developed will it be possible to assess the impact of the ideas fully.

Writers on this topic tend to assume that the monitoring of mental processes in learning requires sophisticated introspection, at a level of the university student or at least adult in style. In this book we have tried to apply the ideas to a younger age group. If learning to learn is to be achieved, the basic patterns must be laid down in early adolescence, or perhaps earlier.

Teachers wishing to tackle these ideas with school-age children

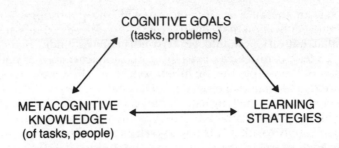

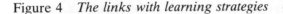

Figure 4   *The links with learning strategies*

might choose to structure their thoughts around a modified version
of the model shown earlier in the book as Figure 2, as it throws up a
number of questions to provoke thought or guide discussion.
Where can teachers intervene in this model to make learning more
effective?

> *Cognitive Goals.* Establish clearer cognitive goals for yourself
> and for the children you teach. Distinguish between outcomes
> and processes of learning. Divide tasks into constituent parts.
> Relate goals to pre-planning and subsequent reflection sessions
> with pupils.
> *Metacognitive Knowledge.* Explore how your own knowledge of
> your learning, the task and the learning context influences
> performance, and share this with pupils by 'modelling'. Allow
> them to explore their own metacognitive knowledge by discus-
> sion and by exposure to a variety of contexts or circumstances.
> *Learning Strategies.* Attempt to discern general strategies used
> across tasks. Distinguish these from skills. In teaching, stress
> these common strategic elements and reinforce their successful
> use where possible. Identify how strategies change in line with
> goals, knowledge and context. Encourage the children to gener-
> ate search procedures or 'trigger' routines that enable them to
> scan and make full use of their available strategic repertoire.

These suggestions are expressed in the technical vocabulary of
cognitive psychology because at present this is the only language in
which they can be stated concisely. The examples in Chapter 7
illustrate ways in which the ideas can be translated into classroom
practices. A teacher prepared to tackle at least some of these issues
will have made a start on the task not just of teaching pupils, but of
teaching them how to learn.

Learning strategies beyond the classroom

This line of thinking accords closely with the philosophy of the continuing education movement. Now, more than ever, it is necessary that education should go beyond instilling knowledge and should seek to foster the capacity to go on learning. A poll of employers' views on the qualities sought in their new recruits (reported in the national press on 12 December 1984) put 'ability to learn' at the top of the long list: employers want 'graduates who are trainable rather than trained'. Many of the principles discussed in this book apply to adult learning as well as to children's education.

For adult learners, 'reflection' may be a more helpful and less technical term than 'metacognition'. In *The Reflective Practitioner*, Schon (1983) analysed how professionals think in action (the subtitle of his book) and identified reflection as a means of improving professional judgment:

> Competent practitioners . . . often reveal a capacity for
> reflection on their intuitive knowing in the midst of action and
> sometimes use this capacity to cope with the unique, uncertain
> and conflicting situations of practice.

'Reflection' is also the term used by Boud, Keogh and Walker (1985) in a collection of essays on learning, representing a process comparable to metacognition but more general. This process is 'of central importance in a variety of teaching and training contexts', enabling us to draw out the learning potential from our experiences. In one of the chapters in this book, Main (1985) discusses how to assist students to learn more effectively:

> The most productive ways . . . have been those in which
> students reflect critically on their own practices rather than
> through prescriptions of 'good' learning practice.

The capacity to reflect critically and to respond flexibly in learning can be developed by adults if they recognise the need for it. In this way they will more effectively manage their own learning. At present, however, the need often goes unrecognised, except at certain critical stages, such as the approach of examinations or entrance to careers, or when returning to learning as a mature student. Even then, short courses of instruction in techniques of study are a poor substitute for a continuing education throughout the years of schooling. Our argument is that the best point to start is when children's developing cognitions are matched by a degree of self-awareness which allows them to begin to explore their learning strategies.

Bibliography

Anderson, L. (1981), *Student Responses to Seatwork: Implications for the Study of Students' Cognitive Processing*, Research Series No. 102, Institute for Research on Teaching, Michigan State University.

Baird, J.R. and White, R.T. (1982), 'Promoting Self-Control of Learning', *Instructional Science*, 1982, 11, 222–247.

Baird, J.R. and White, R.T. (1984), 'Improving Learning through Enhanced Metacognition: A Classroom Study', Paper given at the meeting of the American Research Association, New Orleans, April 1984.

Baird, L.L. (1983), *Review of Problem-Solving Skills*, Research Report, Princeton, Educational Testing Service.

Baron, J. (1978), 'Intelligence and General Strategies', in G. Underwood (ed.), *Strategies of Information Processing*, London, Academic Press.

Barrs, M. (1983), 'Born Again Teachers – A Review of the Work of Donald Graves', *TES*, 24th June 1983, p. 23.

Bereiter, C. and Anderson, V. (1975), *Thinking Games*, Book 2, The Ontario Institute for Studies in Education, Occasional Paper 16.

Beveridge, M. and Dunn, J. (1980), 'Communication and the Development of Reflective Thinking'. Paper presented at the Annual Conference of the Developmental Section of the BPS, University of Edinburgh.

Boud, D., Keogh, R. and Walker, D. (1985), *Reflection: Turning Experience into Learning*, London, Kogan Page.

Britton, J. (1972), *Language and Learning*, London, Penguin.

Brown, A. L. (1974), 'The Role of Strategic Behaviours in Retardate Memory', in N.R. Ellis (ed.), *International Review of Research in Mental Retardation*, New York, Academic Press.

Brown, A.L. (1977), 'Development, Schooling and the Acquisition of Knowledge about Knowledge', in R.C. Anderson, R.J. Spiro and W.E. Montague (eds), *Schooling and the Acquisition of Knowledge*, Hillsdale, N.J., Erlbaum.

Brown, A.L. (1978), 'Knowing When, Where and How to Remember: A

Problem of Metacognition', in R. Glaser (ed.), *Advances in Instructional Psychology*, Hillsdale, N.J., Erlbaum.

Brown, A.L. (1980), 'Metacognitive Development and Reading', in R.J. Spiro, B. Bruce and W.F. Brewer (eds), *Theoretical Issues in Reading and Comprehension*, Hillsdale, N.J., Erlbaum.

Brown, A.L. and Campione, J.C. (1977), 'Training Strategic Study Time Apportionment in Educable Retarded Children', *Intelligence*, 1, 94–107.

Brown, A.L. and Campione, J.C. (1979), 'Inducing Flexible Thinking: The Problem of Access', in M.P. Friedman, J.P. Das and N. O'Connor (eds), *Intelligence and Learning*, New York, Plenum.

Brown, G. (1984), 'Metacognition: New Insights on Old Problems?', *British Journal of Educational Studies* (in press).

Brown, J.S. (1983), 'Learning by Doing Revisited for Electronic Learning Environments', in M.A. White (ed.), *The Future of Electronic Learning*, Hillsdale, N.J., Erlbaum.

Bruner, J.S. (1965), *The Process of Education*, Cambridge, Harvard University Press.

Bruner, J.S., Goodnow, J.J. and Austin, G.A. (1956), *A Study of Thinking*, New York, Wiley.

Butterfield, E.C. and Belmont, J.M. (1977), 'Assessing and Improving the Executive Cognitive Functions of Mentally Retarded People', in I. Bailer and M. Steinlicht (eds.), *Psychological Issues in Mental Retardation*, Chicago, Aldine Press.

Cavanaugh, J.C. and Borkowski, J.G. (1980), 'Searching for Metamemory-Memory Connections: A Developmental Study', *Developmental Psychology*, 16, 5, 441–453.

Cavanaugh, J.C. and Perlmutter, M. (1982), 'Metamemory: A Critical Examination', *Child Development*, 53, 11–28.

Cockburn, A. (1983), 'The Quality of Pupil Learning Experience', *Link*, Spring 1983, University of Lancaster, Centre for Educational Research and Development.

Dansereau, D. (1978), 'The Development of a Learning Strategies Curriculum', in H.F. O'Neil (ed.), *Learning Strategies*, New York, Academic Press.

Dearden, R.F. (1976), *Problems in Primary Education*, London, Routledge & Kegan Paul.

Donaldson, M. (1978), *Children's Minds*, Glasgow, Fontana.

Duffy, G.G. (1982), 'Fighting off the Alligators: What Research in Real Classrooms has to say about Reading Instruction', *Journal of Reading Behaviour*, vol. XIV, No. 4, 357–373.

Durkin, D. (1979), 'What Classroom Observations Reveal about Reading Comprehension Instruction', *Reading Research Quarterly*, vol. XIV, 4, 481–533.

Entwistle, N. (1981), *Styles of Learning and Teaching*, Chichester & New York, Wiley.

Entwistle, N. and Wilson, J.D. (1977), *Degrees of Excellence: The Academic Achievement Game*, London, Hodder & Stoughton.

Feuerstein, R. (1979), *The Dynamic Assessment of Retarded Performers*, Baltimore, Maryland, University Park Press.

Flavell, J.H. (1970), 'Developmental Studies of Mediated Memory', in H.W. Reese and L.P. Lipsitt (eds), *Advances in Child Development and Behaviour*, New York, Academic Press.

Flavell, J.H. (1976), 'Metacognitive Aspects of Problem Solving', in L.B. Resnick (ed.), *The Nature of Intelligence*, Hillsdale, N.J., Erlbaum.

Flavell, J.H. (1981), 'Cognitive Monitoring', in W.P. Dickson (ed.), *Children's Oral Communication Skills*, New York, Academic Press.

Flavell, J.H. and Wellman, H.M. (1977), 'Metamemory', in R.V. Kail and J.W. Hagen (eds), *Perspectives on the Development of Memory and Cognition*, Hillsdale, N.J., Erlbaum.

Francis, H. (1985), 'Individual Differences in Reading Ability – A New Perspective', in C. Bagley and G. Verma, *Festschrift for Philip Vernon* (in press).

Frederiksen, N. (1983), *Implications of Theory for Instruction in Problem Solving*, Research Report, Princeton, Educational Testing Service.

Galton, M. and Simon, B. (eds) (1980), *Progress and Performance in the Primary Classroom*, London, Routledge & Kegan Paul.

Galton, M., Simon, B. and Cross, P. (1980), *Inside the Primary Classroom*, London, Routledge & Kegan Paul.

Galton, M. and Willcocks, J. (1983), *Moving from the Primary Classroom*, London, Routledge & Kegan Paul.

Gibbs, G. (1977), 'Can Students be Taught How to Study?', *Higher Education Bulletin*, 5(2), 107–118.

Gittins Report (1967), *Primary Education in Wales*, London, HMSO.

Graves, D. (1983), *Writing: Teachers and Children at Work*, London, Heinemann.

Hamblin, D.H. (1981), *Teaching Study Skills*, Oxford, Blackwell.

Hirst, P.H. (1965), 'Liberal Education and the Nature of Knowledge', in R.D. Archambault (ed.), *Philosophical Analysis and Education*, London, Routledge & Kegan Paul.

Holt, J. (1964), *How Children Fail*, New York, Dell Publishing Co.

Hopson, B. and Scally, M. (1980), *Lifeskills Teaching Programmes*, Book 2, Maidenhead, McGraw-Hill.

Kirby, J.R. (ed.) (1984), *Cognitive Strategies and Educational Performance*, London & New York, Academic Press.

Lawson, M. (1980), 'Metamemory: Making Decisions about Strategies', in J.R. Kirby and J.B. Biggs (eds.), *Cognition, Development and Instruction*, London, Academic Press.

Laycock, S.R. and Russell, D.H. (1941), 'An Analysis of 38 How-to-study Manuals', *School Review*, 49, 370–9.

Light, P. (1979), *The Development of Social Sensitivity*, Cambridge,

Cambridge University Press.

Light, P. (1983), 'Social Interaction and Cognitive Development: A Review of Post-Piagetian Research', in S. Meadows (ed.), *Developing Thinking*, London, Methuen.

Lunzer, E. and Dolan, T. (1979), 'Reading for Learning in the Secondary School', in C. Asher (ed.), *Language, Reading and Learning*, Oxford, Basil Blackwell.

Maddox, H. (1962), 'An Analysis of How-to-study Manuals (Abstract)', *Bulletin of the British Psychological Society*, 47, page A29.

Maddox, H. (1963), *How to Study*, London, Pan Books.

Main, A. (1985), 'Reflection and the Development of Learning Skills', in D. Boud, R. Keogh and D. Walker, *Reflection: Turning Experience into Learning*, London, Kogan Page.

Marland, M. (1981), *Information Skills in the Secondary Curriculum*, Schools Council Curriculum Bulletin 9, London, Methuen.

Mathematics 5–11 (1979), HMI Series, Matters for Discussion, 9, London, HMSO.

Meichenbaum, D. and Goodman, J. (1971), 'Training Impulsive Children to Talk to Themselves: A Means of Developing Self-control', *Journal of Abnormal Psychology*, 77, 115–126.

Monroe, W.S. (1924), *Training in the Technique of Study*, Bulletin 20, Bureau of Educational Research, University of Illinois.

Mugny, G., Perret-Clermont, A. and Doise, W. (1981), 'Interpersonal Co-ordinations and Sociological Differences in the Construction of the Intellect', in G.K. Stephenson (ed.), *Progress in Applied Social Psychology*, Vol. 1, London, Wiley.

Nisbet, J. and Shucksmith, J. (1984), *The Seventh Sense*, Scottish Council for Research in Education, Edinburgh. Also in *Scottish Educational Review*, 16, 75–87, November 1984.

Norman, D.A. (1973), 'Memory, Knowledge, and the Answering of Questions', in R.L. Solso (ed.), *Contemporary Issues in Cognitive Psychology: The Loydla Symposium*, Washington, D.C., Winston.

Phenix, P.H. (1964), *Realms of Meaning*, New York, McGraw-Hill.

Piaget, J. (1928), *Judgement and Reasoning in the Child*, New York, Harcourt Press.

Piaget, J. (1932), *The Moral Judgement of the Child*, London, Routledge & Kegan Paul.

Plowden Report (1967), *Children and Their Schools*, London, HMSO.

Resnick, L. (1981), 'Instructional Psychology', in *Annual Review of Psychology*, 32, 660–704.

Resnick, L. and Beck, I.L. (1976), 'Designing Instruction in Reading: Interaction of Theory and Practice', in J.T. Guthrie (ed.), *Aspects of Reading Acquisition*, Baltimore, Md, Johns Hopkins University Press.

Robinson, E. (1983), 'Metacognitive Development', in S. Meadows (ed.),

Developing Thinking: Approaches to Children's Cognitive Development, London, Methuen.

Robinson, E.J. and Robinson, W.P. (1982), 'The Advancement of Children's Verbal Referential Communication Skills: The Role of Meta-cognitive Guidance', *International Journal of Behavioural Development*, 5, 329–355.

Robinson, F.P. (1946), *Effective Study*, New York, Harper.

Rubinstein, M.F. (1975), *Patterns of Problem Solving*, Englewood Cliffs, Prentice-Hall.

Russell, J. (1981), 'Dyadic Interaction in a Logical Reasoning Problem Requiring Inclusion Ability', *Child Development*, 52, 1322–5.

Russell, J. (1982a), 'Cognitive Conflict, Transmission and Justification: Conservation Attainment through Dyadic Interaction', *Journal of Genetic Psychology*, 140, 283–97.

Russell, J. (1982b), 'Propositional Attitudes', in M. Beveridge (ed.), *Children Thinking Through Language*, London, Edward Arnold.

Scardamalia, M., Bereiter, C. and Fillion, B. (1981), *Writing for Results: A Sourcebook of Consequential Composing Activities*, Curriculum Series 44, The Ontario Institute for Studies in Education.

Schallert, D.L. and Kleiman, G.M. (1979), *Some Reasons why the Teacher is Easier to Understand than the Textbook*. Reading Education Report Series, Center for the Study of Reading, University of Illinois.

Schon, D.A. (1983), *The Reflective Practitioner: How Professionals Think in Action*, London, Temple Smith.

Siegler, R.S. (1978) (ed.), *Children's Thinking, What Develops?*, New York, Wiley & Sons.

Silbereisen, R.K. and Claar, A. (1982), 'Stimulation of Social Cognition in Parent-child Interaction: Do Parents make use of Appropriate Interaction Strategies?' Paper given at conference on New Perspectives in the Experimental Study of the Social Development of Intelligence, Geneva.

Simon, H.A. (1973), 'The Structure of Ill-structured Problems', *Artificial Intelligence*, 4, 181–202.

Smith, R.M. (1983), *Learning How to Learn: Applied Theory for Adults*, Milton Keynes, Open University Press.

Spencer, E. (1983), *Writing Matters across the Curriculum*, Kent, Hodder & Stoughton.

Sternberg, R.J. (1983), 'Criteria for Intellectual Skills Training', *Educational Researcher*, 12 (2), 6–12.

Tabberer, R. and Allman, J. (1983), *Introducing Study Skills: An Appraisal of Initiatives at 16+*, Windsor, NFER-Nelson.

Tenney, Y.J. (1975), 'The Child's Conception of Organisation and Recall', *Journal of Experimental Child Psychology*, 19, 100–114.

Truscot, B. (1946), *First Year at the University*, London, Faber.

Vygotsky, L.S. (1962), *Thought and Language*, New York, Wiley.

Waterhouse, P. (1983), *Supported Self-Study in Secondary Education*,

Working Paper 24, London, Council for Educational Technology.

Waters, H.S. (1982), 'Memory Development in Adolescence: Relationships Between Metamemory, Strategy Use and Performance', *Journal of Experimental Child Psychology*, 33, 183–195.

Wellman, H. (1977), 'Preschoolers' Understanding of Memory-relevant Variables', *Child Development*, 48, 1720–1723.

Wellman, H.M. (1981), 'Metamemory Revisited', Paper presented at Social Research into Child Development, April 1981, Boston.

Yussen, S. R. and Bird, J.E. (1979), 'The Development of Metacognitive Awareness in Memory, Communication and Attention', *Journal of Experimental Child Psychology*, 28, 300–313.

Index of authors

Subject index